Wendy!
Rock Your Profits

How to be a Finance Rock Star

How to be a Finance Rock Star

The Small Business Owner's Ticket
to Multi-Platinum Profits

Nicole Fende, A.S.A.

Small Business Finance Forum
Cheyenne, WY

This book is designed to provide accurate and authoritative information about small business finance. Neither the author nor the publisher is engaged in legal, accounting, tax, or financial services by publishing this book. If any such assistance is required, the services of a qualified professional should be sought. The author and the publisher will not be responsible for any liability, loss, or risk incurred as a result of the use and application of any information contained in this book.

© 2012 by Nicole Fende

All rights reserved. No portion of this book may be reproduced, stored in a retrieval system, or transmitted in any from or by any means – electronic, mechanical, photocopy, recording, scanning, or other – except for brief quotations in critical reviews or articles, without the prior written permission of the publisher.

Small Business Finance Forum, LLC
109 E 17th Street
Suite #63
Cheyenne, WY 82001

www.smallbusinessfinanceforum.com

First printing, February 2012
ISBN 978-0-9837659-0-5

Library of Congress Control Number: 2012901691

Cover Design: Cynthia Levesque, Cynthia Creative & Co.
Mascot & Villain Illustrations: Jennifer "Scraps" Walker, Helper Monkey Designs
Author Photo: Sarah Morreim, Sarah Morreim Photography

This book is dedicated to my husband Paul.

TABLE OF CONTENTS

Foreword by Carol Roth — ix
Introduction — 1

SECTION 1: CHORDS & MELODIES

Chapter 1: Kicking Stage Fright in the A** — 9
Tips and Tricks to Tame Your Fear of Finance

Chapter 2: Set Your Multi-Platinum Profit Goals — 21
So You Want to be a Rock-n-Roll (Business) Star?

Chapter 3: The Simple Formula to Achieve Your Goals — 27
Unlock the Secret with Just Four (4!) Numbers

SECTION 2: MAKING THE BAND

Chapter 4: Busking to Barter — 39
Creative Ways to Fund Your Business

Chapter 5: The Quarter Conundrum — 55
Can't Buy Me ~~Love~~ Success

Chapter 6: Time is Money Baby — 63
The Hidden Price of Free

Chapter 7: Stop Burning Money — 69
Is your Lack of Expense Management Burning Down The House?

SECTION 3: WHAT'S YOUR CUT?

Chapter 8: Pricing Principles — 83
Dirty Deeds (Should Never) Be Done Dirt Cheap

Chapter 9: Pricing Multiple Products — 97
Bands Sell More Than Music

Chapter 10: Discounts, Promotions and Upgrades 105
Don't Upgrade Your Business into Failure

SECTION 4: HITTING THE STAGE

Chapter 11: Viva Las Vegas 111
Business is a Gamble - Stack the Odds to Win

Chapter 12: We Will Rock You! 123
It's Showtime - Turning Your Plan into Profit

Chapter 13: (Don't be) Dancing on Your Own 133
Stagehands, Managers and Roadies

Chapter 14: Surviving Glitter 137
Even Multi-Platinum Singers Make Mistakes <u>and</u> Comebacks

APPENDIX: CURTAIN CALL

Finance Rock Star Playlist 143
pbSmart™ Codes 149
Kiva.org 151
Rock Star Resources 153
Index 155
About the Author 159

FOREWORD

Over my career, I have helped companies raise over $1 billion and successfully complete around three quarters of a billion dollars in mergers and acquisitions transactions. This has given me unparalleled access to peek behind the curtain and look at how companies manage their financials.

What I have seen- from companies big and small- is two things. First, there's a desperate lack of comprehension surrounding financial statements at all levels in companies of almost every size. Second, this lack of comprehension costs businesses significant money and opportunities, and in some cases, causes financial ruin. This book gives you the tools to ensure that neither of these will ever apply to you or your business again.

What I love about this book is that it takes concepts in and around finance, which can be both boring and complex, and makes them easy to understand (and, gasp, sometimes even fun)! Nicole Fende has a gift for breaking down these topics and that gift is rooted in experience. Nicole- like me- has a background as an investment banking analyst. She has spent her career building financial statements from the ground up for companies in a variety of industries and understanding the ins and outs of not only financials, but also the analysis of them that makes them useful tools to small business owners. The book is light in tone and broken into easy to comprehend chunks- a welcome departure for a finance book.

Several years back, I encountered a company that built their business up to $10 million in revenue and back down to almost nothing because of financial mismanagement. I had another client that grew revenue in a haphazard manner and took a $5 million in revenue business making $1 million in profit a year to one that made more than $20 million dollars a year, but was losing money (aka had no profit to show). The decisions these management teams and CEOs made in their businesses were based on assumptions about, rather than the reality of, their financial statements.

Whether you are a financial novice who thinks that a turnover ratio is the portion of an apple turnover that you have to share with your significant other, or if you are more comfortable with financials, but don't know how to analyze your business for constant improvement, you will find a lot of value in the following pages. They are broken down in an easy to follow manner, so that you won't get overwhelmed in the process.

Who knows, you may even laugh a few times too.

Wishing you much success.

Carol Roth

Business Strategist (CarolRoth.com) and New York Times Bestselling Author of *The Entrepreneur Equation*

INTRODUCTION

If you're a small business owner, solopreneur, freelancer or entrepreneur-to-be who fears finance and avoids numbers, this book is for you. If you want to plug your profit black holes and grow your bottom line, this book is for you. If you are searching for a book that will explain finance in plain English, this book is for you. If you like to laugh (and who doesn't?), this book is for you!

As my small business consulting practice grew, I realized that there was a hunger for easy to apply, easy to understand, finance information. Surprisingly, the demand was for this information to be delivered in a creative, quirky manner, preferably with a few good jokes thrown in.

This need was tailor made for me, The Numbers Whisperer™.

- ☆ **Technical know-how?** I'm a credentialed actuary - Associate in the Society of Actuaries (A.S.A.). *Check.*

- ☆ **Practical experience?** My career has literally spanned the globe, and includes a role as Chief Financial Officer, as well as an Investment Banker. *Check.*

- ☆ **Ability to translate Financese to English?** Not only do my clients give rave reviews, online my guest posts are in high demand because they are relatable and clear. *Check.*

- ☆ **A Sense of Humor?** Heck if you don't laugh at least once while reading this book I'll eat my pocket protector. Uh-oh, did I just admit I have a pocket protector? *Check.*

Given the constraints of time and space, I realized a book would be the best way to reach the broadest audience. I'm passionate about showing small business owners and entrepreneurs that *finance doesn't need to be hard, scary, or dry as the desert.*

Of course the minute someone says finance people shut down. But Rock Star? Who doesn't want to be a Rock Star? You'll see the theme throughout, and I've even included a Playlist in the Appendix.

This book is broken down into four sections. While each chapter was written to be an independent lesson for ready reference, keep in mind the earlier chapters form the building blocks for later exercises.

Section 1: Chords & Melodies

All music requires basic building blocks; chords and melodies are the foundation upon which any rock star builds. Of course all the knowledge in the world is useless if you can't get on stage and play.

This section starts with simple and effective ways to **move past your fear of numbers.** Then you'll learn how you can **use only four numbers** to understand what drives profit in your business and **unlock the secret to multi-platinum profits**.

Section 2: Making the Band

Once you've got a handle on the basics you need to finance your band and decide how to spend your (limited) resources. Of course somebody in the band also has to manage the money and track expenses.

This section starts with **creative (lesser known) ways to fund your business** such as; crowd funding, barter, customer funding, joint ventures, sponsorships, peer to peer lending and more.

Once you get some cash you need to decide how to spend it. Recklessly throwing it at the first ideas to cross your inbox isn't a path to success. In Chapter 5 you'll learn how to **evaluate the return on money spent** for a new expense or initiative. This tool will give you an objective, easy to understand analysis of your options.

In Chapter 6 we will explore the most undervalued asset of any business. Learn a quick and easy way to ensure that it's spent wisely. A Finance Rock Star uses all their assets to full advantage.

Then it's time to **tame the budget beast and earn an instant 35% return**. Learn how you're burning money, how to stop it today and an easy system to fix the problem for good.

Section 3: What's Your Cut?

In this section you will learn **how to set prices for your products that will generate the profit you desire**. Remember, revenue doesn't necessarily equal profit. It's important to know what your cut is from each product or service you sell.

This easy to follow and easy to implement process will transform your pricing. No more guessing games. No more wishing and hoping for the results your business needs to succeed.

Discover if sales and promotions are the black hole sucking all the profits out of your business. **Learn how to run a profitable sale or promotion**, one that will generate buzz, please customers, and still deliver the bottom line your business needs.

Section 4: Hitting the Stage

The stage is set, the stadium is full, and the band is ready. It's time to take this show live!

Running a business, even with a carefully crafted plan, is a risk. **The key to success is stacking the odds in your favor.** The first chapter in this section introduces you to a simple, yet effective tool to manage your risk and resources while pursuing your profit goals.

Then it's time to set your Key Metrics. **Learn how to create a business scoreboard that reports on your performance in a glance.** Business is a competition, and you want to win.

Rock Stars travel with a whole smorgasbord of people. They have stage managers, roadies, grips, lighting experts, sound techs and more. As awesome as you are, you too need help for some things in your business. **This chapter covers when to get help and how to find it.**

Understand how to track progress and make needed course corrections. Even superstars make mistakes. **Learn how to bounce back and be more successful than ever.**

The Illustrations

As you read, you'll meet a cast of characters created for this book. Jennifer "Scraps" Walker is the amazing talent behind these illustrations, bringing my vision to paper with ESP-like skill. However it wouldn't be fair of me to credit her with the silly, clearly Photoshopped images. That's all me.

Why? Why include silly, obviously Photoshopped images in my book? Good question! There's a reason, more than one actually.

- ☆ Finance is a topic that's easy to get frustrated with. You feel like you're wrestling an octopus on steroids. Not fun. These images are there to remind you not to take any of this too seriously.

- ☆ When you look at the Photoshopped images you can see my message. It may not be as pretty or glossy as the latest gossip mag, but it's effective. When you use the tools in this book they may not seem glossy, but they are effective.

- ☆ Rock Stars break the rules.

QR Codes

QR Codes is the abbreviation for Quick Response Codes. They are the next generation in barcode technology, originally developed in Japan as a means of managing and tracking inventory.

Today QR Codes have gone mainstream, you see them on mailings, in brochures, even the grocery store! They offer a powerful and cost effective way for small businesses to reach their target market.

Watch me now!

Here's how to use the QR Codes in this book. You will need a smartphone to access them. Go to the application (apps) website for your phone. Search for a QR Code reader and install on your phone. Once it is installed just point your camera phone at the QR Code to "read" it.

If you don't have a smart phone you can still access these bonus items. *You can find a list of all the links on the Finance Rock Star website at* http://www.FinanceRockStar.com/book/qrlinks.html.

I've had the pleasure of working with pbSmart™ Codes by Pitney Bowes to develop the QR Codes for this book. A huge thank you for opening my eyes to the world of possibilities QR Codes offer to small businesses. As you access the special features in this book, consider how you might use the same options to reach and connect with your target market.

Let's Rock!

SECTION ONE
Chords & Melodies

All music requires basic building blocks; chords and melodies are the foundation upon which any rock star builds. Of course all the knowledge in the world is useless if you can't get on stage and play.

This section starts with simple and effective ways to **move past your fear of numbers**. Then you'll learn how you can **use only four numbers** to understand what drives profit in your business and **unlock the secret to Multi-Platinum Profits.**

CHAPTER ONE
Kicking Stage Fright in the A**

Think big stars don't get stage fright? Think again! Some of the most famous names in music have dreaded getting on stage in front of a live audience. Jim Morrison, John Lennon and even tough guy rapper, Eminem, all suffered excruciating performance anxiety.

Worried that you can't achieve Finance Rock Star status because the mere thought of numbers makes you nauseous?

Fear not! I've put together a list of the most common fears and symptoms a budding Finance Rock Star faces, and how to tackle them quickly and easily.

Mom's Spaghetti

In Eminem's break out song, "Lose Yourself", he talks about how hard it is to keep down mom's spaghetti before an important show. It's tough to discuss any topic when you feel like you're about to empty the contents of your stomach. That's why I invented **Finance Dramamine**.

Finance Dramamine is guaranteed to treat that awful nauseous sensation, letting you focus on the numbers without distraction. Even better, there are no pills to swallow or pesky wristbands to wear.

Take out a piece of paper and in large print write something similar to one of the following items:

☆ Big Client just paid $100,000

☆ Bank Balance is $1,000,000!

☆ My Paycheck this week was $10,000

Hang that piece of paper over your desk. Look at it every day and say **"THOSE are numbers I like to see."** You might also try something like this:

Think this is silly?

I understand, because when I was first introduced to the technique by Dr. Shannon Reece, my reaction was "Really? Come on..."

Then I discovered something: <u>it works</u>.

Finance and numbers are simply tools to reach your profit goals. Write down your profit goal numbers, and post them in a place where you'll see them every day.

After all, isn't making a profit why you have your own business?

Behind the Floodlights

When you step onto a stage you often can't see beyond the floodlights. Not knowing what's out there is scary.

Think about Stephen King, the undisputed champion of horror.

His books focus on fear, often deep rooted ones, encouraging your imagination to run wild. That's why the movies never live up to his books. The movies give a face to the fear.

Suddenly it doesn't seem so scary anymore.

We want to mimic the Stephen King movie effect!

The easiest way to do this, **create an avatar**.

Let me introduce the **Number Muncher**, my villain avatar. His favorite pastime is to tear up people's financials.

While you wouldn't want him hanging around the office, Number Muncher looks *manageable*.

Prefer something closer to a horror movie? How about this guy?

He doesn't have a name, I just think of him as my axe murderer: a serial murderer who targets small business profits.

He'll pop up throughout the book, drawing your attention to key pitfalls that can attack your profits and even kill your business.

The Underwear Option

I know that in days past, screaming fans would throw their undergarments on stage. That's not quite where we're going here.

There's an old public speaking tip that tells you to imagine the audience in their underwear when you get nervous. Next time a nervous speaker starts smirking you *know what's going through their head.*

Where was I? Underwear!

Imagine your avatar in its underwear. Yes; it's that simple, and I bet it will make *you* smirk. Try it with my axe murderer right now. Made you smile didn't it?

Learn from Jim Morrison

Any Doors fan will tell you that Jim Morrison was so filled with stage fright he began his career singing with his back to the audience. Morrison never truly faced his fears, instead relying on drugs and alcohol to temporarily remove them.

Sadly, those addictions led to his untimely death at a young age.

Failing to face your fear can be fatal to your business. The first step in conquering them is answering one simple question.

What's your real fear?

I know, I know. You're going to say finance, numbers, or even Excel.

Maybe not.

When I work with profit coaching clients I often hear,

> *"That's a relief. I was worried that my business couldn't meet my profit goals."*
>
> *"I was afraid my prices would have to be much higher."*

By avoiding the numbers, they were really avoiding a related fear. Such as, "I'm afraid to go to my friend's house... her dog bit me last time I visited."

What's your real fear?

Let's take a look at common finance related fears.

THE METEOR

Otherwise known as *The End of the World*. A fear of impending **DOOM**.

This event is something you can't control, can't stop and can't fix. You may think, well, heck, if I can't change it why think about it?

I can give you two reasons:

1. Most likely there IS something you can do, it just may not be obvious or easy. <u>You can't figure it out if you don't think about it.</u>

2. On the teeny tiny chance the world is ending, wouldn't you want to know so you don't waste your time on a business that won't exist in a month?

FYI - If I ever learn a meteor is hitting the earth I'm having a HUGE party.

Yes you're invited.

STICKER SHOCK

Ever gone to buy a ticket for a popular act and been shocked by the cost? I know I have!

When I'm approached by a new client for pricing help they often inform me that I can't "make their prices outrageous".

And here I was, planning on suggesting a minimum price of an arm and a leg.

You need to know if your prices will create the income you desire.

The great news is that there ARE solutions to this other than raising prices. We'll be covering them in Chapters 3, 10 and 11.

GOBBLEDYGOOK

Back in the 80's there was a parenting group that insisted if you played certain vinyl records backwards you could hear a message to worship the devil.

I listened to these so-called devil messages, all I heard was a bunch of gobbledygook. Basically what you would expect to hear listening to *anything* backwards.

I can appreciate that without a background in math, accounting or finance, doing the books or other types of analysis may be intimidating. I get the shivers every time I'm faced with writing new sales copy.

Start with the easy stuff, like your business bank account. Seek out resources that use plain English rather than overly technical terms.

Build your knowledge today to grow your bank balance tomorrow.

WHAT WILL THEY THINK?

They might think I look stupid if I ask that question. High school may be long ago; however, that fear of looking bad in front of others lives on.

So who're ***they*** anyway? If they're your friends they won't think you're stupid. If they're your direct competitors let them think you're stupid, then they'll underestimate you. As for the general masses, I hate to tell you, they just don't care.

One other thing to consider: What would make you look more stupid, asking a question or going out of business?

BRIDGE OUT

Have you ever wondered how someone could actually drive off a bridge with all the signs, the flashing lights, and yes, even barricades?

It does happen. Don't believe me? Just Google it.

Do you harbor a secret fear that you aren't on the right track? Do you fear you're headed off an unfinished bridge instead of happily cruising on the road to riches?

It's not too late. Instead of ignoring your business finances, take a look, and you might just see the detour to success.

The Mascot

Help Wanted: Sidekick / Mascot

In the first few tips we talked about horror movies. While I may be an aficionado of hack and slash, I realize others prefer comedy, action, and the ubiquitous buddy movie.

Unless you live under a rock (in which case, where do you plug in your PC?), you're familiar with sports teams and mascots.

I had the um, well, luck? to marry into a college football obsessed family. Yes, my husband's family loves Badger Football. For the unitiated, that's the University of Wisconsin and the Badger is their ~~god~~ mascot.

Every time Wisconsin scores, Bucky the Badger does one push-up for each point. When things are going poorly, he leads the cheering. Even I can't imagine a Wisconsin football game without Bucky.

A Mascot is a touch point, a rallying point and a cheerleader.

Who wouldn't want one?

Meet **Fluffy the Finance Feline**, the official mascot of Small Business Finance Forum.

Cute, cuddly and quick to pounce on profits, Fluffy is great to have around.

Not a cat person?

Meet Maxine, the Math Mutt.

Max can sniff out any difficult profit problem. She doesn't take any bull and is very loyal.

Who would make a great mascot for *your* finances?

Since Fluffy and Maxine have both mastered the art of being in two places at once, feel free to use either of them as your finance mascot.

Buddy Up

Why are buddy movies so popular?

They're relatable. We all have buddies. In your life it may be a running buddy, travel buddy, dating buddy (a.k.a. Wingman) or even a buddy to watch cheesy subtitled martial arts films with.

Now it's time to get yourself a Finance Buddy.

It's ok if your finance buddy doesn't like numbers either. Think about Scooby Doo and Shaggy; they might both be scared of ghosts but they still solve the mystery!

You can cheer each other on and keep each other honest (did you really review last month's expenses?).

Bringing Sexy Back

Finance can be Sexy!

Really. Finance can be sexy.

Before you get too carried away, I'm NOT talking beer commercial sleazy sexy. Think Victoria's Secret instead of Fredericks of Hollywood. James Bond over Chippendales.

You get the idea. Back to finance!

Let me show you the sexy side of finance.

LITTLE BLACK DRESS

Every woman has her version of the LBD (Little Black Dress). It's her go to dress, the one she never feels fat in. The one she knows will knock the socks off those fortunate enough to be around her.

In order to be sexy, Finance needs her own little black dress (hey it's my imagination at work here, and I say Finance is a woman).

The real magic of the LBD is its Mojo, the sense the wearer has that she looks amazing. We want to create that feeling for you when you approach finance.

We need to create a strong visual of what you want to accomplish financially. Next time your Mojo is failing, think about that image.

Here are some ideas for that visual:

- ☆ Jumping into a pile of money (watch any Vegas movie for this one)
- ☆ Watching a movie in the home theater of your custom built house
- ☆ Sitting on a private yacht being served Mimosas at brunch

Take five minutes right now and create a compelling mental picture to embody your financial goals.

SPORTS CAR

Don't sexy people drive sexy cars?

Heck yeah!

I must confess a long standing love of fast cars, especially muscle cars.

Who wants to be all dressed with no way to get to the party?

We need a way to get there... ***in style****.*

Like most finance people, I love spreadsheets. I'm guessing you're ambivalent at best, and probably cringe at the idea of opening up Excel.

Spreadsheets are a necessary part of achieving your goals. *Yet there's no reason to ride in the uncomfortable, one step above a tin can, version.* That's what basic Excel is like. Riding in a sub-compact car with no AC on a hot day. **YUCK.**

Did you know in Excel you can:

- ☆ Include images. Big ones, small ones, maybe some of that private island you plan to buy.
- ☆ Add color anywhere - fonts, cell colors, border colors and more
- ☆ Create useful and colorful graphs that tell you important things at glance.
- ☆ Add music (who knew right)?
- ☆ Add YouTube Video clips!

Take a deep breath, and dive into Excel just to play. Yes, play!

Go experiment in Excel right now. Try inserting images, adding color, or including a YouTube video.

Be Cool

All Rock Stars are cool.

Think of your favorite lead singer, bass guitarist or drummer. They stay calm in a tough situation. They don't overreact. They wear sunglasses all the time (you can skip that one).

Most importantly . . . they get what they want in the end.

In the book, *Right Brain Business Plan,* author Jennifer Lee talks about Chill Pills. They're ways to relax when you're frustrated or overwhelmed by your business.

My favorite Chill Pill is going for a run. It clears my head, letting me focus on a solely physical task. When I get back (and shower!), I'm very effective.

Your Chill Pill may be another form of exercise, or it may not involve it at all. Some swear by meditation, others like to watch a bit of TV. Studies have shown that 20 minute naps can actually give you a great boost!

Your Chill Pill will be as unique as you are. Just remember to take it!

CHAPTER TWO
Set Your Multi-Platinum Profit Goals

When someone wants to become a famous musician they have a specific goal, such as *Top Country Singer*, *The Next P-Diddy*, *Best New Folk Singer*, or *Greatest Elvis Impersonator Ever*.

Yes *Make Money* is a goal, but it's too general to be effective.

Can you imagine an Elvis Impersonator showing up for a Hip Hop Video casting call? He's probably not going to get the job. Now imagine that same singer auditioning for a Las Vegas casino lounge act. His odds of success just went through the roof!

What if your business made one dollar?

You just reached your goal. Yes, with one dollar in profit you just reached your goal of *making money*. Not ready to celebrate yet? You *might* be able to buy a candy bar with it, then again you might not.

What about a billion dollars? Sure, but that's not a realistic goal.

In 2011 the band U2 had the top grossing concert tour raking in $195 million. By anyone's calculation those are definitely multi-platinum profits. Yet U2 formed in 1976! It takes time to reach your full potential (although not necessarily 35 years).

Step 1: Setting Your Income Goals

Income goals can and should change over time. Most startup businesses don't earn a profit in the first year, or even the first couple years. As Carol Roth points out in her book, *The Entrepreneur Equation*, the word "scheme" usually follows "get rich quick".

Max's No Bull Corner

Revenue ≠ Profit

A company can have millions, even billions in revenue and still lose money.

Yet a company that brings in only 1 million in revenue can generate a profit of $100,000 or more!

Which company would you prefer to own?

Setting unrealistic goals helps no one, and is generally a path to failure. It's fine to dream big, just accept that it won't all happen tomorrow.

Your income goal is the amount you expect your business to deposit into your personal bank account after all business expenses are paid.

Think of it as your salary. If you were doing the same thing for someone else, what would you expect them to pay you?

Now answer the same question for the following year, and the year after that. For simplicity I'll refer to the next twelve months as Year 1, the following 12 months as year 2, and so on. This doesn't mean it's the first year you're in business, it's simply the first year in your current business plan.

Considerations in Setting Your Income Goals

Start-ups and young businesses
- ☆ What do you need to earn to meet all your personal bills and obligations? This makes a good objective for Year 2 or Year 3.
- ☆ You would expect rapid income growth in the early years of a business. Be sure you have a concrete plan on how to achieve it.
- ☆ Seek out successful mentors, preferably in your market. Get their input on your goals. A great place to connect with experienced professionals (for free) is Score.org.

Established businesses
- ☆ Established businesses should strive to grow profits at the rate of inflation or higher. While this can vary over time, I recommend to my coaching clients a minimum of 5% per year.
- ☆ Even established entrepreneurs tend to pursue aggressive growth goals. As with start-ups, be sure to create a realistic plan on how.
- ☆ Insider Info – Find out (legally!) about the competition with these free resources; www.BizStats.com and www.SBA.gov.

Time to Write Down Your Income Goals

Year 1 Income Goal: _____
Year 2 Income Goal: _____
Year 3 Income Goal: _____
.
.
Year 10 Income Goal: _____ *(Your Multi-Platinum Profit Goal!)*

Step 2: Setting Your Work Week Goals

Everyone would love to work five hours a week and be a billionaire. Perhaps your desire is "simply" to live the life of a rock star. Look behind the hype and you'll see that rock stars work very hard to achieve success and live their glamorous lifestyles. Real sustainable wealth requires real sustainable work.

Yet working 100 hours every week isn't desirable either. Creating work life balance is important to the long term success of any entrepreneur.

I *need* my tuna break.

Consider musical artists whose success has spanned decades, such as Bruce Springsteen, Madonna, The Rolling Stones and U2. They all have outside interests. Yes, they work hard, but not every week. They have friends and families, they support charities, and they pursue interests not related to music.

Striking a balance, and understanding how the time commitment will change as your business grows is essential. Lady Gaga is a great example (the singer who wore a meat dress to the MTV Awards). When Lady Gaga releases a new song *now* the press, the coverage, and the buzz are instantaneous. Her celebrity insures a certain degree of publicity making it much easier to market her new releases.

However, when she first started, Lady Gaga had to work incredibly hard just to get noticed. In addition to wearing raw meat, (I can only imagine the smell after a few hours) she had to fight for every second of coverage. The time she needs to spend now to generate buzz is substantially less than when she first started her career.

The distinction between short-term goals and long-term goals is crucial.

When working with my coaching clients, or those enrolled in my *Rock Your Profits* online course, I recommend assuming at least 40 hours per week when first starting a business. Realistically it's closer to 50 or 60 for a start-up. <u>Make 40, or less, your long-term goal as the business matures</u>.

Step 3: Setting Your Vacation Goals

I love taking vacations: beach vacations, ski vacations, family vacations, overseas vacations . . . well you get the idea. Unfortunately, many entrepreneurs put off taking a vacation, even one that involves nothing more than hibernating in front of your TV, and catching up on episodes of your favorite show.

They worry about what will happen while they're gone. They worry about what opportunity may be missed, or what detail overlooked. Learn from David Lee Roth, formally the lead singer of Van Halen. He discovered this important fact the hard way.

No one is indispensable, not even you.

Model yourself after musical artists whose success has spanned decades. While these artists work hard when they have a new album or tour to promote, they also take breaks and have even said recharging enables them to come back revitalized. Their breaks infuse new creativity and energy, fueling their continued success.

Madonna is a great example. In 2010 she ranked as the 8th highest paid musician, earning a reported $58 million (Forbes). Yet she's nowhere to be seen on the list in 2011. Why? Because she took a break after promoting her latest album and an intense worldwide concert tour.

As when setting the number of hours per week you plan to work, consider both short and long term goals. It's not healthy or recommended to work 52 weeks a year, just like it's not good to work 100 hours every week. On the other hand it's not realistic to expect to work three weeks a year and earn six figures.

When working with my coaching clients, or those enrolled in my *Rock Your Profits* online course, I recommend assuming no more than 50 weeks per year, then stick to it! Make 48, or less, your long-term goal as the business matures.

CHAPTER THREE
The Simple Formula to Achieving Your Goals

The secret to unlocking your profits can be found in four numbers and one easy formula. You've already got the first three numbers;

- Annual Income Goal
- Hours Worked Per Week
- Weeks Worked Per Year

So what's missing?

The percentage of time you spend on profit generating tasks.

This crucial fourth number is often overlooked by small business owners, yet it can mean the difference between success and failure. Once entrepreneurs have a firm handle on this number, they can pinpoint why they haven't achieved their profit goals despite strong revenue numbers.

The cold hard reality is that you don't earn money every hour you're working. There are activities and tasks that you must perform that aren't revenue generators. For example, you must file your taxes. However, taxes cost you money, they don't make you money. Your business needs to be licensed appropriately, have the right legal structure, and solid contracts and documentation.

No one pays you to do these administrative tasks.

Yet, if you don't pay taxes or follow applicable laws, it will cost you money and may even land you in jail.

Rock 'n Roll stars can get away with having a mugshot. Willie Nelson, 50 Cent, Billie Joe Armstrong (Green Day), and even Johnny Cash all had great careers after getting arrested. In some circles, it may have even given their sales a boost!

For small business owners, though, this is most definitely not good for business.

Therefore, business owners with the strongest profits have found ways to complete the necessary administrative tasks in the least amount of time. That's why your **Efficiency Ratio** is the fourth, and perhaps most important number, in the formula for success.

Your **Efficiency Ratio** is the percentage of total hours worked that are spent on income generating activities. Examples include performing services for a client, creating a product to sell, or any other activity that can be billed to a client.

To get an accurate picture of your current efficiency it's crucial to count <u>everything</u>, every hour worked, every administrative task completed.

I know it's a pain, but at the risk of sounding completely cliché, "No pain, no gain."

Are you in business to make money or to be comfortable? If you answered "to be comfortable," I suggest you invest in a good armchair and give up the idea of running your own company.

> **If you don't count all your activities then you are WORKING FOR FREE.**
>
> Activity brainstorming list to get started:
> - Performing service for a client
> - Time spent on Social Media Interaction – Twitter, Facebook, LinkedIn, etc.
> - Setting up a client in administration system
> - Continuing education or new skill set training
> - Creating products to sell
> - Invoicing clients
> - Creating sales and marketing materials for your business
> - Time spent reading and answering emails
> - Bookkeeping

When I first discuss the Efficiency Ratio with clients I often get estimates of 80%, 90% or even 95%. The likelihood of this being true is about equal to the likelihood that I'll wake up tomorrow with a voice like Susan Boyle. *Hint: babies fall asleep in self-defense when I sing.*

I'm not saying that people are being deliberately dishonest; they're simply unaware of how they actually spend their time. I bet you're in the same boat.

Consider putting on a rock show; the time to practice, to set up for the show, the after show stage tear down, the drive from one show to the next. Do you really think that they spend 80% of their time or more actually performing a show?

Performing the show is a rock star's revenue generating activity.

Setting up the stage, practicing beforehand and travel time, those are all things that aren't revenue generating. A band could practice 80 hours a week. If they never perform, they'll never get paid.

> **EASY LITMUS TEST**
>
> *Is someone paying you to do it?*

A realistic assumption is between 60% and 70%. **In fact I often recommend people start with 50%.** Why is that? Well, in big consulting firms, where every minute is tracked and efficiency is king, the gold standard is 70%. If consulting companies, which have every incentive and plenty of resources to increase efficiency, believe 70% is a home run grand slam, do you really believe that you can do better?

Don't believe me? **Take the Big Brother challenge.** RescueTime.com is a service that will track and report on exactly how your time is spent. It runs silently in the background, tracking all your activities without getting in the way. It will even ask what you've been doing when your computer is idle for a long period of time.

RescueTime.com offers both free (Solo Lite) and paid versions. Run it for a week and then tell me I'm wrong.

If in setting your goals for the upcoming year you assume an increase in efficiency, be sure to have actionable plans or goals that should deliver improved efficiency. Otherwise your pricing will be too low, and won't achieve your profit goals.

There are many ways to improve efficiency which is good news for you and your bottom line. This will be covered in more detail in Chapter 6.

Time to Calculate

Yes I said that dreaded word – calculate. Calculations of course include numbers and (gasp) a formula! Lucky for you I'm The Numbers Whisperer™. Numbers are more like your family pet than a scary monster. I'm going to show you how to teach them to do all the cool tricks, and avoid the stinky mess untrained puppies make.

$$\left(\begin{array}{c}\text{Annual}\\\text{Income}\\\text{Goal}\end{array}\right) \div \left(\begin{array}{c}\text{Hours}\\\text{Per}\\\text{Week}\end{array}\right) \div \left(\begin{array}{c}\text{Weeks}\\\text{Per}\\\text{Year}\end{array}\right) \div \left(\begin{array}{c}\text{Efficiency}\\\text{Ratio}\end{array}\right)$$

Take a deep breath, it really is *easy*. Let's do an example so you can see for yourself. We'll make the following assumptions:

- Annual Income Goal = $100,000
- Hours Working Each Week = 40 hours
- Weeks Working Each Year = 50 Weeks
- Efficiency Ratio = 50%

Now put it into the formula. **Just plug and play like the Rock Star you are!** It's as easy as learning the three chords used in every Ramones song.

$$\left(\$100{,}000\right) \div \left(40\text{ Hours}\right) \div \left(50\text{ Weeks}\right) \div \left(50\%\right)$$

The answer is $100.

You may be wondering…

What Does It Mean?

This is the amount you must earn, net of all expenses, for every hour you spend on revenue generating activities.

If you're a **service provider,** this number represents the minimum you must earn for each billable hour you work in order to achieve your income goal.

Using our earlier example, you would need to earn $100 per hour to reach your annual income goal of $100,000.

The result you get from this formula is the amount of money that must come back to you as profit *after all expenses are paid.*

Service Providers

- Bookkeeper
- Business Coach
- Marketing Consultant
- Sales Consultant
- Social Media Expert
- Web Designer

Since our result was $100, you need to be charging at least *$100 plus expenses per hour* to be profitable. If you charge less than this, you won't achieve your profit goals.

We'll cover more on expenses and pricing in Chapters 7 and 8.

Manufacturer or Producer

- Artist
- Handmade Bath & Body Products
- Handcrafted Jewelry
- Machinist
- Niche Manufacturer

If you **produce or sell a physical product,** this number represents the minimum you must be earning for each hour you spend creating or manufacturing a product in order to achieve your income goal.

Again, the result you get from this formula is the amount of money that must come back to you as profit *after all expenses are paid.*

If it takes you 2 hours to produce one widget, then with our example, you would need to charge $200 ($100*2) plus expenses in order to meet your profit goals. Any less than this and you would fail to earn your target income.

It cannot be stressed enough that this number, this hourly rate, is a minimum. **If you believe the market will bear a higher price, then you should charge it.**

The Local Garage Band Earns More than You

Did you just learn that your products or services are woefully underpriced? Do you suspect the local garage band earns more than you? Are you primed to rush out and increase your prices right now?

My advice – wait.

Wait? Wait she says! I just realized I can't make my profit goals with my current prices. Why would I wait?

I'm not suggesting you wait long, just take the time to finish this book. In the upcoming chapters you may discover:

- ✩ You haven't accounted for all your expenses, which would mean *raising prices again* in a short period of time.
- ✩ Other adjustments in your business will allow you to *keep your current prices*.
- ✩ If you have a variety of products or services *your price adjustment may not be the same* for all of them.

You're not Elton John

Elton John holds the record for the highest average concert ticket price ($306 in 2008 if you're curious). Unfortunately, you're not Elton John. While I never encourage small business owners to make their competitive strategy to be the lowest price, I realize that there are reasonable upper limits on the price they can expect their clients to pay.

Did the result from this formula indicate your prices needs to be 2, 3 or 4 times what you or your competition currently charge? Does this mean you can't earn your target income?

Absolutely not!

It means you need to look at areas you can control to meet your income goals. Here are some common culprits keeping you from your goals. We'll address these later in the book, and the appropriate chapter is noted.

- ✩ Expense structure *(Chapter 7)*
- ✩ Spending 50% or more of your time on administrative tasks *(Chapters 6 & 11)*
- ✩ Pricing your products and services *(Chapters 8 & 9)*

Take heart, even Elton John wasn't charging Elton John prices when he first began his career!

The Stadium Isn't Full

If you're a relatively new business you may be seeing the effects of unused capacity. Just like a new band may not be able to book concerts or shows every night that they're free, you may have free hours in which you'd like to serve clients, but the demand isn't yet there. The cure for this is simply effective marketing and time.

Scan now to get a customized report on your profit drivers. Your answers to a short survey will be used to create an article tailored to your needs.

SECTION TWO
Making the Band

Once you've got a handle on the basics you need to finance your band and decide how to spend your (limited) resources. Of course somebody in the band also has to manage the money and track expenses.

This section starts with **creative (lesser known) ways to fund your business** such as; crowd funding, barter, customer funding, joint ventures, sponsorships, peer to peer lending and more.

Once you get some cash you need to decide how to spend it. Recklessly throwing it at the first ideas to cross you inbox isn't a path to success. In Chapter 5 you'll learn how to **evaluate the return on money spent** for a new expense or initiative. This tool will give you an objective, easy to understand analysis of your options.

In Chapter 6 we will explore the most undervalued asset of any business. Learn a quick and easy way to ensure that it's spent wisely. A Finance Rock Star uses all their assets to full advantage.

Then it's time to **tame the budget beast and earn an instant 35% return**. Learn how you're burning money, how to stop it today and an easy system to fix the problem for good.

CHAPTER FOUR
Busking to Barter

Everyone has seen them. The aspiring musicians who hang out on busy street corners, in subway tunnels and in public parks. They play their hearts out hoping someone will drop a few dollars in their collection bins.

In today's tough economic times, getting the funding necessary to start your business may seem like an impossible task. In fact, you might be looking over at your dusty banjo wondering if there's a good spot open at your local park.

Even if you're the next Eddie Peabody, it's worth considering alternate ways to raise money --that don't involve hanging out in a subway station.

The reality is that **you can grow when cash flow is low**.

In this chapter you'll learn about unique ways to raise cash for your company that don't involve going to the bank. While you may be tempted to pooh-pooh a few, take a second look. A pleasant surprise could await your bank account.

Funding Starts At Home (and eBay)

You're probably sitting on at least a thousand dollars in collectibles and so-called junk. Recently (ok - I admit, it was after watching an episode of *Hoarding: Buried Alive* on TLC) I decided there was simply too much clutter in the house. Some things I donated, while others I decided to list on eBay to see what would happen.

One man's junk IS another man's treasure.

In total, I brought in over $1,100. From stuff. In my house. Stuff that I didn't use or even want. Here are just a few examples of the things I sold:

Watch and learn how to raise money using eBay

- ✯ Antique Spinning Wheel $120
- ✯ Small (used) jewelry box $22
- ✯ Vintage Costume Jewelry (broken!) $50
- ✯ Limited Edition Fitz & Floyd Figurine $135
- ✯ Old beaten up laptop $110
- ✯ Old wireless router $17
- ✯ Unopened Limited Edition CD $32
- ✯ Surplus of unused scrapbooking paper $200+

When listing an item just be clear on its present condition, including any blemishes or marks. Don't assume someone else won't want it. Did you notice that I sold some broken ~~old~~ vintage jewelry for $50?

Of course, there are also collectibles you may have that are simply dust magnets or storage space hogs. Figurines, crystal, discontinued china patterns, old action figures, sports memorabilia, vinyl records, even old toys are bought and sold online every day.

If you have a number of used books to sell, consider listing them on Amazon.com. There's no fee to list, and most of the information is pre-loaded, just fill in the ISBN.

Trade Gold Jewelry for Gold Profits

Unless you never turn on the TV or radio you know the value of gold has climbed substantially in the last few years. Online companies, jewelry stores, pawn shops and rare coin dealers are all offering to buy your unwanted or broken gold jewelry. This can be a great way to quickly generate cash; however, do some research first and select a reputable company that offers a competitive price.

You may have some designer pieces, or something from a high end brand like Cartier or Tiffany. There was even an article by Jean Chatzky in the May 2010 issue of *More Magazine* that discussed selling your jewelry to raise cash.

As Chatzky points out in the article, if you have high-end pieces, it's better to deal with a specialist. The person highlighted in the article ended up receiving *$17,000 for her jewelry!*

Men have hidden treasures, too. Open up your accessory armoire. High end and limited edition watches can demand a good resale price. A Rolex is always more than just a watch.

Broken or unwanted gold cufflinks, tie tacks and chains are perfect fodder to sell. Don't forget your collectible coins, either. Their worth far surpasses the metal alone.

Crowd Funding

Still longing to strum your banjo on a corner? Then crowd funding is for you. *Think street busking meets Web 2.0 (when do we get 3.0 anyway?).*

According to Wikipedia, crowd funding "describes the collective cooperation, attention and trust by people who network and pool their money and other resources together, usually via the Internet, to support efforts initiated by other people or organizations." It may also be referred to as crowd financing or crowd sourced capital.

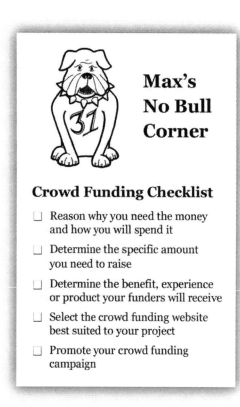

Max's No Bull Corner

Crowd Funding Checklist

- ☐ Reason why you need the money and how you will spend it
- ☐ Determine the specific amount you need to raise
- ☐ Determine the benefit, experience or product your funders will receive
- ☐ Select the crowd funding website best suited to your project
- ☐ Promote your crowd funding campaign

Rough translation of all that financial gobbledygook: getting a group of people who don't know you to fund your project or idea.

What do the people providing the money get out of it?

Crowd funding isn't an investment, and it isn't a charity either. To encourage people to contribute money, creators will offer various products, benefits or experiences to their funders.

The story itself can even be the pull. Many funders are simply intrigued to watch events unfold as someone pursues their dream. Others enjoy being able to say, "I helped make that happen!"

Timing is critical with crowd funding. Many sites will not transfer the funds to you until your goal is hit. In addition, the people committing funds generally have the right to withdraw their support before a project has hit plan.

Here are a few established crowd funding sites, the types of projects they promote, and their associated fees.

- ☆ **Peerbackers.com | RECOMMENDED**
    Anyone with an idea, project, business or invention can apply to post on Peerbackers.com from anywhere in the world. There are no fees unless you reach your funding goal.

    Fees: 5% Success Fee + 2.9% PayPal Processing Fee

    ***VIP BONUS** – Podcast of the Numbers Whisperer™ interviewing Sally Outlaw www.thenumberswhisperer.com/2011/SallyOutlaw/*

- ☆ **Kickstarter.com**
    Focuses on funding creative ideas and endeavors. Perfect for artists, filmmakers, musicians, designers, writers, illustrators, curators, and performers who want to bring their projects, events, and dreams to life.

    Fees: 5% Success Fee + 3 to 5% Amazon Processing Fee

- ☆ **Sellaband.com**
    Musical artists raise funds for music projects (a new album, tour or the promotion of their music).

    Fees: 15% Success Fee

☆ **IndieGoGo.com**
Open for anyone to use, with any type of campaign - creative, cause-related, or entrepreneurial.

Fees: 4% Success Fee + 3% Payment Processing Fee. **WARNING**: If fail to reach your goal, but didn't select the all or nothing option, you'll be charged a fee of 9% plus a payment processing fee of 3%.

☆ **FundAGeek.com**
Exclusively for technical innovation, FundAGeek.com accepts commercial projects based on technology, as well as basic research projects at universities and research institutions.

Fees: 5% or 9% Success Fee + 3% PayPal Processing Fee. The higher success fee applies if you want their Premium Marketing Services.

Turn Groupies into Green (Customer Funding)

Just like groupies can power an independent or unsigned musical group, business groupies can fund your project or start-up. Deadheads (fans of the band Grateful Dead) are a shining example of this.

The Grateful Dead didn't rely on record sales to make money. In fact, they *encouraged* amateur recordings of their concerts by the attendees. The only rule (unspoken but religiously followed), never charge money to share the recordings with others.

This created an intensely loyal following that served as the foundation for an impressive grassroots marketing campaign. The Grateful Dead were able to sell out major professional football stadiums on consecutive nights with no mass-market advertising.

They did this before social media, even before the internet as we know it!

So how did The Grateful Dead make money? From their concert tickets and the sale of tour related swag such as T-Shirts. They relied on their groupies to buy tickets and bring in new listeners. This strategy went against all conventional wisdom, yet made them an undisputed success.

You too can capitalize on groupies, their money, and their influence.

Get business groupies *before* you start singing.

Launching a new restaurant? Offer a VIP Table program only available before you open. This membership could guarantee premier seating, shortest wait or even special discounts once you open. Don't underestimate what people will pay for simple bragging rights.

When I first launched my e-course *Rock Your Profits,* I included a Founding Member component. Founding Members receive a lifetime discount on all my products and services, including consulting. This demonstrates my appreciation and encourages repeat business.

The options and variations are endless. In fact, the more creative and unique your concept the easier it will be to market.

Get your groupies to develop and fund a new product or service.

If you've ever lived in, or even visited, Wisconsin you know that beer drinking is practically an art form there. The same could be said for the way the bars make money. While in Madison, Wisconsin my ~~badger~~ husband brought me to one of the best-known German bars in the area.

When you enter the building, you immediately notice beer mugs of all shapes and sizes hanging from the ceiling above the main bar. Turns out, those mugs belong to patrons. People *paid* for the privilege to hang their mug from the ceiling of the bar. Since the owners limited the number of mugs they would take, they were able to charge more and create bragging rights for their clients.

You can find even more real life examples like these in the book, *School for Startups* by Jim Beach, Chris Hanks, and David Beasley. One of my favorites involves two men, Jim and Doug, who want to start an education program teaching children computer skills at prestigious universities.

To test the idea, they secured space at two key institutes during the summer. That's it. No brochure, no course plan, not even teachers were arranged yet. They started advertising, collecting the results via toll free number and voicemail.

Jim and Doug used the questions and requests from their preliminary advertising to design the course and brochure. They built their initial offering based on the feedback from those first ads! Soon deposits were coming in – it had worked!

Strangers in the Night (Peer to Peer Loans)

What about getting money from a stranger? I'm not talking about loan sharks or your local Godfather.

There are legitimate businesses which connect private lenders with private borrowers. This is commonly referred to as Peer Lending, or Peer to Peer (P2P) Lending.

The benefit to the lenders is the ability to lend directly to borrowers, giving the lenders a higher return. The borrowers can get access to more funds at better rates.

Two established sites to consider for an unsecured business loan are LendingClub.com and Prosper.com.

Remember that P2P Lenders will run your credit if you request a quote.

That's What Friends (& Family) Are For

Borrowing money from friends and family is always tricky. While there's nothing wrong with borrowing from them, you must proceed with caution. Follow these simple rules to ensure you don't ruin your relationship with your family member(s) or friend(s).

- ☆ Don't borrow money unless you'll pay it back in full *even if the business fails*

- ☆ Don't harass, browbeat or whine (my personal nails on the chalkboard!) to get the loan you desire. *Ask once and gracefully accept the answer.*

- ☆ *Be prepared to (nicely!) answer questions about your business*, business plan or business knowledge when you ask for a loan.

- ☆ Be prepared to answer questions from every person to whom you owe money until it's paid back. *They're bound to ask about your business, your progress, even your work hours, and yes, you must still be nice.*

- ☆ Get it in writing. Get it in writing. Yes I mean it, even with your sweet old great grandma – **GET IT IN WRITING!**

If you'd like some online help in raising money from family and friends, or simply need a way to prove to doubting Uncle Thomas that you won't buy beer with your largess, consider using Lendfriend.com or LendingKarma.com.

IPO on Your Terms

Any money in there?

IPO? Is that an iPod Shuffle?

It stands for Initial Public Offering, or the first time a company sells shares to the public.

Traditionally, only large companies working with investment bankers were able to raise money using an IPO.

Today, start-ups and entrepreneurs can also pursue equity investors. However, it's very important to understand exactly what this means to your business and your bottom line.

You're selling partial ownership in your company.

Your investors will own a piece of your company. That means the investors will be entitled to a piece of all future profits. They may also have some input into business decisions and direction. Two online resources to consider:

- ☆ **GrowVC.com**
  Global, transparent, community-based approach to seed-funding. Grow VC can help startups secure initial funding of up to 1M USD for their businesses.

- ☆ **CrowdCube.com**
  If you want to raise money for your business, simply register online and submit your proposal. If it's approved, you'll be able to create your pitch online within minutes and start getting investment for your business. (*Currently available to UK based companies only*).

Duets (Joint Ventures)

Looking to tap into a new market? Perhaps you want to launch a product, service or even new business but lack a certain skill or asset. Rather than hiring someone, consider partnering up to get it.

Before approaching a potential partner, lay out your business plan, including the unique strengths and skills you bring to the table. Decide up front what you're willing to offer in terms of profit sharing to entice the other person to join forces. Be clear why you need each other to make the plan a success.

Avoid have tunnel vision when considering partners. **An unconventional partnership could have far greater benefits than a traditional safe bet.** A great example of this would be the collaboration of Run DMC and Aerosmith back in the 80's to create the hit song "Walk This Way".

At the time the idea of rappers covering a hard rock group was absurd. Yet the song became an international hit, winning both groups a Soul Train Music Award in 1987 (Best Rap Single). It launched an entire musical sub-genre of rap rock, leading the way for artists like Kid Rock.

Sponsorships

Musical tour sponsorships are as common as an Elvis impersonator in Las Vegas. Like Elvis impersonators, there's also a great deal of variety (late Elvis, skinny Elvis, crazy side burns Elvis). Here are a few examples:

- ☆ Red Stag by Jim Beam sponsored Kid Rock's 2009 Tour
- ☆ Van's (the skateboard apparel manufacturer) and Kia were featured sponsor for Van's Warp Tour 2010
- ☆ KC Masterpiece Barbecue Sauce and Kingsford Charcoal sponsored country artist Keith Urban's 2010 Summer Lovin' Tour

- ☆ Bacardi was the official spirit of the Black Eyed Peas E.N.D. Tour in 2010, including the creation of "V.I.Pea", a Bacardi daiquiri
- ☆ U2 asked Clorox to provide a Brita water bar for its 360-degree tour to reduce bottled water consumption by tour staff (Clorox agreed)

Although these were all musical events, each sponsor was as unique as the artist. For example, I can't imagine U2 asking Jim Beam to be a sponsor, nor do I think that Brita would be a good fit for Kid Rock's fans.

To successfully pursue a sponsorship you must first clearly define the market you're serving. (*Hint: Everybody isn't an answer*). The more focused your market, the more believable it becomes. **Try creating a client avatar, an imaginary character that personifies your target market**.

Max's No Bull Corner

Sponsorship Checklist

- ☐ Precisely identify the common ground between your market and the potential sponsor's market
- ☐ Determine the value the potential sponsor can expect to gain from supporting your business
- ☐ Whenever possible offer an option to showcase how your business uses their product or service
- ☐ Create a professional presentation focusing on value to the sponsor and their expected return
- ☐ Use your network (including social media) to get an introduction to your target sponsors

Now ask yourself, what would my avatar be interested in? What would my avatar buy? Who offers those products and services (other than you)?

Take that list and consider which names on it might be a fit. Country music fans are likely to enjoy grilling out, so a tie-up between Kingsford Charcoal and Keith Urban creates a win-win. Use the checklist Max the Math Mutt has thoughtfully provided to prepare a sponsorship pitch.

Barter

Yes barter! Barter gets a really bad rap, and it's completely unjustified. You barter every day. You just use a middle man, commonly referred to as the *Almighty Dollar*.

At some point in history, people realized hauling a big bag of grain around to buy some shoes was a real pain. They needed something to represent that grain that was lightweight and easily identified as having value. Coins were created, and many backs were saved.

Not convinced?

Consider this. You need products from Widgets R Us valued at $200. You write Widgets R Us a check for $200. Widgets R Us needs services from you valued at $200. Immediately after receiving your check, they write one to you for your services for $200.

Sounds pretty silly doesn't it? Bartering simply cuts out the middleman.

Traditional Barter

Bartering with someone you already know is the easiest method. You may be surprised how many people in your direct circle who are open to a barter arrangement. You just need to communicate your needs to them. Like spouses, significant others and the barista at your local coffee shop, your business colleagues don't have ESP. You must speak up.

Approach it professionally. Be prepared to discuss exactly what you're willing to offer, and the current price you charge for that product or service. Indicate what you're seeking from them in exchange. Then allow them a graceful way to turn you down.

The worst that will happen is they say no. Offering a barter opportunity is all upside with no risk. Wouldn't it be nice if more things in business were like that?

The Barter Triangle

Many times when you make the barter suggestion you'll hear, I'm open to barter but what I really need is _____. Unfortunately, that something is not what you offer.

Let's assume you're a writer, and provide various copywriting services. The person with whom you're talking is a local restaurant or coffee shop that has great private meeting rooms you were hoping to use. The owner really needs an accountant.

Is the deal dead? Nope. You just need to complete the triangle. Find an accountant that needs some new marketing materials written or some other service that you offer. Then you can structure a deal where you provide services to the accountant, the accountant provides services to the restaurant, and you get your meeting space.

There are two keys to making this work. First you have to bring together the three points of the same triangle. Then create a written agreement everyone signs before any work begins.

Bartering with Strangers

With the power of the internet bartering with strangers can be done with relatively little risk. There are groups who have married technology with the oldest form of transferring value, barter.

- ☆ ITEX – A Small Business Trading Community
- ☆ IRTA – International Reciprocal Trade Association
- ☆ Bartercard.com – A cashless trading exchange
- ☆ U-Exchange.com – Swap site for just about anything

Barter Ground Rules to Protect Your Profits

- *You must offer something of real value, and it must be the market value.* Don't offer an eBook claiming a value of $300 when you sell it online for $5.

- Treat your partner in barter as you would any other client. *They are a paying client.*

- Expect to be treated as any other client. *You are a paying client.*

- *Get it in writing.* This ensures everyone has the same understanding of expectations. It also enables you to hold people accountable. Finally it provides documentation for the tax man. Which leads to…

- *Don't forget the IRS.* You are still exchanging things of value, commonly referred to as Payment in Kind (PIK). Review any trades with your accountant to be sure all taxes have been paid.

Still Need Money?

If none of these will work for you, don't give up. Innovate!

Keep it legal, ethical, and get it in writing. Who knows, you may end up inventing the next crowd funding.

CHAPTER FIVE
The Quarter Conundrum

You've got some cash. Great! Now what? Suddenly you're overwhelmed with options, ideas and yes, scams. Your budget is not a bottomless pit. You need a way to determine where to spend what you have.

Wouldn't it be nice to have a tool that would give you an objective, easy to understand analysis? Something that wouldn't give you a headache every time you used it? There is!

You may be wondering if this is just a sneaky trick for me to include more calculations. I can assure you they all have a purpose.

Life Lessons at the Grocery Store

Growing up I often accompanied my mom to the supermarket. Occasionally I would be the proud owner of a quarter during this excursion. Back in the days when a quarter actually bought something!

This newfound wealth opened up three distinct options for me. Each had benefits and drawbacks.

Quarter Option #1

Save the quarter until I have more money which would give me more purchasing options – like that new Star Wars figure.

- ☆ Benefits: Retaining the exact value of the quarter.
- ☆ Drawbacks: I wouldn't leave the store with anything new.

Quarter Option #2

Buy a candy bar with my quarter. The store always had my favorite; Reeces Peanut Butter Cups.

- ☆ Benefits: Enjoyment of eating a yummy treat.
- ☆ Drawbacks: The experience is temporary. Once it's gone, it's gone.

Quarter Option #3

Try my luck with the toy dispenser. They were gumball-like vending machines that dispensed toys in small plastic capsules.

- ☆ Benefits: There were always a couple really cool toys you might get from the toy dispenser
- ☆ Drawbacks: This was definitely a risky proposition. Some of the toys in the dispenser weren't even worth a nickel.

Like any kid with money to burn I immediately knew and understood these options. The issue was making up my mind.

Most days I went for the toy dispenser, a high risk / high reward decision.

How does my quarter conundrum relate to your business?

No one has an unlimited budget. Although you have more than the quarter I proudly held in my childhood, you're still operating within certain constraints. You have to decide the best way to spend that money, while considering the benefits and drawbacks or risks.

ROI (Return on Investment) analysis can help you do that.

I barely have enough to cover my marketing campaign, forget about investments.

Investments? I'm not putting money into the market.

I knew she'd sneak in some fancy terms!

Return on Investment (ROI)

Don't let the name intimidate you. ROI is simply the percentage increase or decrease of an investment over a period of time. In other words, how much did you make or lose on the money you spent.

Calculating ROI: (Profit − Cost) ÷ Cost

ROI is easy to calculate, and provides you with an objective number to compare different investment opportunities. Often small business owners are faced with far more options than they can afford to try.

Marketing budgets are a perfect example. A business could double or triple their budget, and still only sample a fraction of the available options.

Case Study: Marketing budget decision using ROI

- ☆ You have a marketing budget of $1,000.
- ☆ You have three options on which to spend your marketing budget.
- ☆ Each one costs $1,000, so you can only pick one.

OPTION #1

Marketing Activity	*Attend a Trade Show*
Cost	$1,000
Expected Profit	$2,000
ROI	100% = (2,000 − 1,000) ÷ 1,000
Risk Level	High
Additional Information	Your company has never attended a Trade Show before. Although your competitors appear to do well at them, it's high risk because it's an unproven way for your company to bring in new business.

OPTION #2

Marketing Activity	*Traditional Media Advertising*
Cost	$1,000
Expected Profit	$1,250
ROI	25% = (1,250 − 1,000) ÷ 1,000
Risk Level	Low
Additional Information	Your company has successfully used Traditional Media Advertising in the past to bring in new business. However the return per dollar invested is lower for this option.

OPTION #3

Marketing Activity	*Online Pay Per Click (PPC) and Social Media Advertising*
Cost	$1,000
Expected Profit	$1,500
ROI	50% = (1,500 − 1,000) ÷ 1,000
Risk Level	Medium
Additional Information	Your company has dabbled in using PPC & Social Media. Although the overall new business generated was good, the results have been inconsistent and unpredictable. That has resulted in a medium risk for this option.

We've got three options, but we can only pursue one. ROI gives us the ability to make a quick comparison. *Be sure to include the risk level in your comparison.*

	Option 1	Option 2	Option 3
Marketing Activity	Attend a Trade Show	Traditional Media Advertising	Online PPC & Social Media
ROI	100%	25%	50%
Risk Level	High	Low	Medium

Think back to my quarter conundrum. I selected the toy dispenser, the high risk / high reward option. In this marketing budget example Option #1 is the toy dispenser. *But which is the right one for your business?*

It depends. That's not a cop out. **The answer depends on your current circumstances, and it can change over time.**

If this is your entire marketing budget for the year, it would be wise to stick with Traditional Media for a stable, low risk return this advertising cycle. You may get a higher return with the Trade Show, but you may also get a big fat zero. Can your company afford the loss?

Perhaps you have enough current clients you can afford to take some risk. Then you might consider Option 3, where returns are higher but somewhat unpredictable.

As your budget grows, say to $2,000 you might combine the Trade Show with Traditional Media. This offers upside without the risk of losing all your money.

Spending your marketing budget becomes a mix and match game, allowing you to play with different potential scenarios and risks. *The key to making this work is to quantify both the ROI and the Risk Level.*

Two is Better than One

Another way to calculate profit is Internal Rate of Return (IRR). IRR is similar to ROI (Return on Investment). It will tell us the return we make per dollar invested.

Why do we need TWO ways to analyze the same thing?

Quite simply, time. ROI is great when you're looking at the same, relatively short time period; generally a year or less. IRR is best when you need to compare the return on your money over different time periods, or periods longer than a year.

Not convinced? Let's look at two offers with the same risk level.

- *Offer #1:* Invest $1,000 and receive a payout of $1,200.
- *Offer #2:* Invest $1,000 and receive a payout of $1,500.

If we calculate the ROI of both options, it appears that Offer #2 is better with a return of 50%. Before you pull out your check book and take the second offer, consider the following information.

- The payout for Offer #1 is made at the end of 12 months.
- The payout for Offer #2 is made after five years.

Are you still convinced that Offer #2 is the best investment? Let's see what the IRR would be on these two options.

- Offer #1 IRR: 20%
- Offer #2 IRR: 8.4%

In Offer #2, because we have to wait five years to receive the payout, we are only earning 8.4% per year. That's a far cry from Offer #1 which will give us a return of 20% in one year.

Calculating IRR

Although IRR is not as easy as ROI to calculate, there are many options available. Spreadsheet software, such as Excel, includes a plug and play function for IRR. If you find that intimidating, try out our VIP Bonus. A free, easy online calculator created by The Numbers Whisperer™.

VIP BONUS – *Internal Rate of Return (IRR) Calculator*
www.thenumberswhisperer.com/IRR/IRR.html

Time to Choose

Here's a quick chart to help you determine if you should use ROI or IRR when analyzing the return you expect on an investment.

- ✩ *Short Periods of Time* - Use ROI
- ✩ *Over Same Short Period of Time* - Use ROI
- ✩ *Periods of Time Longer than One Year* - Use IRR
- ✩ *Comparing over Different Periods of Time* - Use IRR

CHAPTER SIX
Time is Money Baby

What is the return you earn on time invested? I'm not talking about the time that your clients pay you for. I'm talking about the time you spend doing administrative tasks, creating a DIY website, or customizing a free service for your needs. *You may think, well my time is mine, right?*

Yes and no.

Yes, you own all your time, and no, you don't need to pay someone else for it.

But your time is an asset. *Your time has value*, so how you spend it determines if your return is more or less than its value.

Time is your most precious and irreplaceable asset.

How you invest your time will directly impact your bottom line. Unlike other assets, you can't save it up for a rainy day. Like a phone plan without rollover minutes, you must use it or lose it. Nor can you buy more time. You get twenty four hours in a day and seven days in a week, like every other business owner out there.

Concerned this is getting a bit philosophical? You probably could care less about the esoteric properties of time. I bet in the back of your mind you're thinking, "*I want to be Rock Star, not a Buddhist Monk!*"

Fear not!

You won't be asked to sit cross legged staring at your navel or hike up a mountain to talk to some old guy (what could he know anyway? There's not even internet up there!)... where was I? You won't be required to fill out forms in triplicate or ponder the meaning of the universe.

Time to Get Yo ~~Groove~~ ROTI On

It's time for us to discuss your **Return on Time Invested** (ROTI). You already have all the tools, now you just need to see them in action.

Let's take a common small business start-up scenario and apply ROTI.

Often, entrepreneurs decide to build their own websites from scratch. A DIY site gives the owner complete control over the structure, the layout, behind the scenes SEO (Search Engine Optimization), and more. No waiting for an outside firm to update the site. No risk of looking like 50 other sites because a common template was used.

Sounds great, right? Maybe it even sounds like something you've considered. Website nirvana for free – or so you think.

Have you considered the following?

- ☆ What FTP will you use? Do you even know what that is?
- ☆ Do you know any HTML? Do you need to?
- ☆ Have you ever created your own CSS file?
- ☆ Do you think a WordPress plugin involves an electrical cord?

You're smart. I'm sure you're *able* to learn all these things. The real question is, how long will it take? Let's assume it would take you 160 hours, or one month, to learn these things and build your own site.

Think back to Chapter 3 where you calculated the value you need to earn for one hour of work. In our sample calculation, we determined a net hourly rate of $100. If you paid yourself a fair market value while building your site from scratch, the cost would be $16,000 ($100 per hour * 160 hours). $16,000!

Doesn't sound like a bargain any more does it?

But that isn't a full ROTI analysis. Before embarking on this DIY adventure, you request proposals from a handful of reputable web development firms. You learn that it would cost roughly $7,000 for someone else to create the website of your dreams.

If all the "bids" were outside consultants, the answer is easy, hire the firm quoting $7,000!

Hold it right there. *You don't actually have to pay yourself.* So why spend the cash on an outside consultant? Good question.

First, and most importantly, **if you do it yourself, you'll miss out on the chance to earn $16,000.** If you had been doing work for a paying client you would have brought in $16,000. Of course that means you need to pay someone else to build your site. Yet *even after paying an outside firm $7,000, you would be ahead by $9,000 ($16,000 revenues - $7,000 third party fees).*

While an increase of $9,000 in net profit is compelling, there are even more reasons why you should consider outsourcing.

☆ **Time to Completion**
An expert is going to be able to complete a project faster than a beginner. If you need to hit a deadline, outsourcing can make the difference between success and failure.

☆ **Expertise**
While your result may be "good enough," an expert will bring all their tools, tricks and insights to the table. Think about all the insights and skills you deliver to your clients.

☆ **Better than cloning**
Yes, I confess to a deep love of sci-fi movies, but this is a hard-boiled fact. You can't do two things at once. By outsourcing, you can ensure two things are getting done at the same time, in a professional manner. *This can accelerate how quickly you'll hit certain revenue and profit goals.*

"So if the math makes sense should I always outsource?"

It depends.

That's not a cop out. It's the reality of doing business.

There are certain circumstances in which you may still wish to build it yourself. You may just be starting out, and simply don't have the capital available. You may not be established enough to use that time serving profitable customers. Each business is unique.

That's fine, just recognize that you're essentially paying yourself less than market, and ramp up time to profitability will be longer.

This approach also holds for reviewing so-called free resources and services. What if your time was an asset recorded in your financial statements? Would you be embarrassed by how it's being spent?

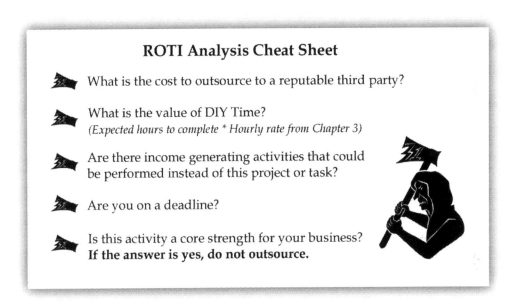

ROTI Analysis Cheat Sheet

- What is the cost to outsource to a reputable third party?
- What is the value of DIY Time?
  *(Expected hours to complete * Hourly rate from Chapter 3)*
- Are there income generating activities that could be performed instead of this project or task?
- Are you on a deadline?
- Is this activity a core strength for your business?
  If the answer is yes, do not outsource.

Bottom line, your time has value. Spend it wisely.

CHAPTER SEVEN
Stop Burning Money

Pop Rock Quiz: What do Jerry Lee Lewis, MC Hammer, and Toni Braxton have in common?

Answer: They have all declared bankruptcy.

No matter how much money you make, you can lose even more. Despite being successful musicians, each of these artists had expenses that dramatically exceeded their income. *No business can afford to ignore their expenses.*

If you were walking down the street and saw a five dollar bill on the sidewalk would you pick it up? Of course you would! Then why are you walking by all that money in your business?

Learn more about how you're burning money every day. Use the QR Code on this page to watch this compelling video.

Did you know that for every dollar of expense you don't track you're losing $1.35?

When you perform work for a client, or produce a product for a customer you incur certain expenses. Let's say you have to buy a Superstar Widget, and it costs $10. Aren't you going to include that cost in the price you charge your client?

If you don't (and why wouldn't you?), you're spending money that should go into your personal bank account for a client's expense. If you don't record the expense you can't ensure you bill the client for it.

Consider this. When you worked for someone else, and had to buy something for your employer with your own money or credit, did you get reimbursed? Of course you did! So why aren't doing the same thing with your business? If you don't treat your business as a business you'll forever be held back from reaching your profit goals.

Where does the other $0.35 come from? Quite simply, the tax man.

From the government's point of view, since you didn't record that dollar of expense, it must be a dollar of income. That means it's taxable! A US business owner is considered self-employed, therefore he or she must pay 12.4% FICA and 2.8% Medicare on their income. Right there you're out 15.2 cents.

What about the other 20 cents? The small business owner in America easily pays more than a 20% tax rate on their earned income between state and federal taxes. In other countries the rates are often higher. At a minimum you're out $1.35 total, it could be much higher depending on your tax bracket.

Give yourself an instant 35% return. Track all your expenses!

Ahoy Matey!

Pirates and Rock Stars have a lot in common. They chase their dreams. They live an adventurous life. **They both pursue gold fanatically.**

I don't know anyone who bounds out of bed in the morning exclaiming, "Yippee! Today I'm going to do my business budget!"

However, if you thought you were on a quest for buried treasure, wouldn't you be excited?

Today we are going on a Treasure Hunt. It just happens to be in your business.

You Need a Map

The first thing a pirate needs to find buried treasure is a map. You need something to help you find all your business gold, something that will make finding your treasure easy.

Is that even possible? Could any finance, numbers thingy actually be easy?

Yes! By investing a little time and energy each month you can make "doing the books" and "running the numbers" an easy task.

I often discover my coaching clients are trying to manually track their expenses. Their desks are buried under a pile of paper, and their receipts have taken on a life of their own. Taming the paper beast is overwhelming.

This would be similar to a pirate ditching his map and digging for treasure at random. Eventually, he might find the treasure. More likely, he'll just give up in frustration.

Help is here. I've got your business treasure map.

There are easy to use tools available which will do 90% of the work for you, and they'll fit into any budget.

- **Shoeboxed.com (US based)**
  Shoeboxed takes your receipts and organizes them into an electronic data file. *You can submit your expenses just about any way you want short of carrier pigeon.* Electronic receipts can be emailed, scanned copies of receipts can be uploaded for processing, and hard copy receipts can be submitted in the postage paid envelopes supplied. I use this and love it.

- **Keebo.com (UK based)**
  Similar services offered as Shoeboxed.com, however they are based in the UK instead of the US.

- **Expensify.com**
  If you have employees take a look at this. They offer a reimbursement option with their paid plan

- **Neat.com**
  Some business owners prefer to scan in their own receipts rather than mail them in for processing. Neat Receipts sells specialized scanners for the DIY entrepreneur.

Try setting aside 30 minutes each week to do something with your finances. Set a timer and let yourself stop when it buzzes. You'll be amazed at how much you accomplish.

Remember, for every dollar of expense you fail to track you're losing $1.35. Expenses left off the budget, or excluded from your pricing analysis weigh your business down. They act as a ball and chain, preventing you from achieving your profit goals.

Yo Ho Ho and a Bottle of Rum

Pirates and Rock Stars both love a good party.

When you plan a big party, wedding or other major event you're actually using a variety of complex expense concepts. From Super Bowl Blowouts to Baby Shower Bonanzas, *you were practicing to be a Finance Rock Star*!

In your business, just like planning that big bash, you want to plan well so you don't overspend or (horror!) run out of some crucial supply during the event. Can you imagine hosting a Super Bowl party that runs out of beer before halftime?

In order to accurately predict expenses, they must be classified.

Think about genres of music for a minute. When you listen to rock music you expect to hear electric guitars. With rap you expect rhyming lyrics spoken, not sung. With classical music you expect clarinets and violins.

Expenses are like music genres. Once we classify them, we can have a good idea what to expect.

Have Your Cake (and Budget Too!)

To help you with categorizing your expenses, think back to a party you helped organize.

Here are some examples to get you started:

- ✩ Baby Shower
- ✩ Bachelor(ette) Party
- ✩ Birthday Party
- ✩ Bridal Shower
- ✩ Engagement
- ✩ Holiday Party
- ✩ Poker Night
- ✩ Retirement Party
- ✩ Super Bowl Bash
- ✩ Wedding

Have one in mind? Good.

Expenses can be broken down into three main categories; variable, step and fixed. We're going to tackle them one at a time, drawing a comparison to some expense or supply from your party that behaves in a similar way.

Red, Red Wine (Variable Expenses)

Every person at a party consumes some type of beverage. For each additional person that attends, additional beverages are needed. There's a direct relationship between the number of attendees and the number of drinks required.

This is a perfect example of variable expenses. No matter how big your party, this expense will stay the same per person.

Let's assume on average each person at a Super Bowl party consumes five beers. If ten people attend the party you would need 50 bottles of beer. If there are 100 people you'll need 500 beers.

What are some common variable expenses in business?

- ✩ **Time**

    There's often a certain amount of time required by you or an employee to deliver a service or manufacture a product.

- ✩ **Commissions**

    Whether your sales are generated internally, or through a third party, your agents will expect to receive the same commission for this first sale as their 500th sale.

- ✩ **Materials**

    This is the easiest to include in pricing. It doesn't matter how many or how few you sell. The material requirements will be constant for each product or service you offer.

Step by Step (Step Expenses)

While most parties don't warrant a Martha Stewart style spread, they generally have food of some kind. Food requirements increase when the guest count increases, but it's not a one to one relationship.

Let's take pizza as an example.

We'll assume that on average one person would eat 3 slices of pizza during a party. Most pizza is cut to have 8 slices.

Therefore you can feed 2.67 people with one pizza (8 ÷ 3 = 2.67).

Have you ever met a 0.67 person?

Here's an example of how to handle the situation.

Let's assume you have 9 people coming to your Super Bowl party. That means you'll need 27 slices of pizza (9 people * 3 slices each = 27 slices).

Stop Burning Money

You'll need 3.375 pizzas to feed everyone (27 slices ÷ 8 slices per pizza = 3.375 pizzas). Unless things have changed dramatically since I went to college, Domino's will not deliver 37.5% of a pizza.

What will you do? If you only get three pizzas, there won't be enough. If you get four pizzas, you'll have leftover pizza. Of course you're going to go with four pizzas, because if people are hungry they'll leave the party.

Good news, a friend calls to say they can come after all. That means you'll have a total of 10 guests. Will there still be enough pizza? You'll need 30 slices to feed everyone (10 people * 3 slices each = 30 slices). That would require 3.75 pizzas (30 slices ÷ 8 slices per pizza = 3.75 pizzas).

You're in luck, four pizzas will be enough.

Even though the number of guests increased, our expense (pizza) did not. Of course, if our expected headcount went up to twelve or more we would need to order another pizza.

Why are they called Step Expenses? Because when you graph them on a chart, it looks like a set of steps.

Headcount is the single most common step expense in business. You won't need to add a new employee every time you add a new client, so it's easy to see how it correlates to our pizza example. Keep in mind, that even if you stretch yourself, you'll probably have capacity when you first add the new employee.

This can be difficult to incorporate in pricing because you need a clear understanding of when to step up, and a fairly accurate prediction of expected sales.

Stuck on You (Fixed Expenses)

These are the expenses you have before the first client is won, and after the 1,001 client is won. You may also hear them referred to as overhead, G&A (general & administrative), or flat expenses.

We're going to head back to our party one more time. What are expenses that were incurred simply because there was a party?

Possible examples include: decorations, a Margarita machine, Karaoke equipment, even Pay Per View Costs (think UFC). Hopefully a citation for noise was not on your list!

What if you decided a Margarita machine would make your party perfect? Whether one person showed up or one hundred people came, the cost to rent the Margarita machine would be the same. Think of this expense as the cost of doing business.

Common fixed expenses include:

- ✩ Annual report filing fees for the states in which you do business
- ✩ Annual Marketing Budget – even your Pay Per Click (PPC) budget because there's no guarantee any of those clicks will become sales
- ✩ Errors & Omissions Insurance for the year

The easiest way to determine if it's a fixed expense is to ask two questions.

1. Would I have this expense even if I have no clients?
2. Will this expense stay the same even if I grow by 100% this year?

If you answered yes to both, it's a fixed expense.

Fixed expenses are easy because you know what they will be for the year. Yet they are hard because you need to allocate them appropriately to your projected sales. If you overestimate sales, you could end up losing money because your pricing doesn't reflect enough Fixed Expenses

Stop Burning Money

Congratulations! Your expenses are now classified by genre, fixed, step and variable. This is a huge step towards meeting your profit goals. Now it's time to use those classifications to predict what is in store for the upcoming year.

For this we are going to consult our crystal ball. Of course pirates have crystal balls, they're great swag.

Wouldn't you like to know your expenses for the coming year?

You can! That's how we are going to get to the final X on the map, and enjoy our business treasure.

Predicting the Future

At the beginning of this chapter we discussed ways to make tracking your expenses easy. Using the data you've collected, sort your expenses into the three main categories; variable, step and fixed. This will be the baseline for our projections.

Predicting Your Fixed Expenses

- ☆ Review the past year's expenses, and remove any that will not occur in the coming year. Equipment purchases are a good example of non-recurring expenses.
- ☆ Will you have new types of expenses this year? Be sure to add them.
- ☆ Account for the growth of your fixed expenses. All expenses grow over time. At a minimum use inflation for your expense growth.

Don't fall victim to the same trap as many big corporations. They convince themselves they can "manage their costs" only to realize at the end of the year they were wrong. *Everyone is affected by inflation.*

Fixed Expense Projection Mistakes

⚑ Failing to include all fixed expenses

⚑ Failing to include new fixed expenses

⚑ An expense growth rate that is too low

Predicting Your Variable Expenses

The key to accurately projecting variable expenses is to understand the main driver. *Most companies have expenses that are based on revenue.*

Commissions are a perfect example. Let's say the commission rate is 10%. This percentage is constant no matter if have the business has sales of one dollar or one million dollars. The expense will be 10% of revenue.

Generally, variable expenses calculated as percentage of revenue are fairly constant. Unless you have made significant changes to the underlying expense structure, you can use the same percentage in your projections.

Companies often have a second type of variable expense that is not related to revenue. You may have expenses based on the number of products or services sold. Perhaps each time you sell a service, there are $100 in administrative fees. It doesn't matter if the price of service is $1,000 or $100,000, there's an administrative fee of $100 each time the service is sold to a client.

The administrative fee itself is likely to change, with similar growth assumptions as your fixed expenses. In this example, assuming an inflation rate of 5%, you would use $105 as the administrative fee each time a new service is sold to a client.

Predicting Your Step Expenses

Step expenses, like pirates, can be tricky.

As mentioned earlier, employee salaries are the most common step expense. When projecting step expenses you must understand what drives the increase. Is it revenues? Number of products sold? Something else?

Let's assume our employee step expense is driven by the number of products we sell. For every additional 500 products we sell in a year, we will need to add another employee.

Thinking back to our party example:

- ☆ Employee salaries = Pizza
- ☆ Number of Products = Expected guests at party

If we expect our sales to exceed 500 in the coming year, we need to plan to add another employee. If we expect our sales to exceed 1,000 in the coming year, we need to plan to add two new employees.

Celebration

What pirate, or rock star, doesn't love a good party?

Have you finished with a stack of receipts? Finally automated your invoicing? Or projected your expenses for next year?

Then it's time to celebrate!

Aren't you likelier to start sooner and finish faster if you know a reward is in store for you? It doesn't have to be big or expensive, just a little something extra for a job well done.

SECTION THREE
What's Your Cut?

In this section you will learn **how to set prices for your products that will generate the profit you desire**. Remember revenue doesn't necessarily equal profit. It's important to know what your cut is from each product or service you sell.

This easy to follow and easy to implement process will transform your pricing. No more guessing games. No more wishing and hoping for the results your business needs to succeed.

Discover if sales and promotions are the black hole sucking all the profits out of your business. **Learn how to run a profitable sale or promotion**, one that will generate buzz, please customers, and still deliver the bottom line your business needs.

CHAPTER EIGHT
Pricing Principles

Every rock band has three basic components; a singer, a guitarist, and a drummer. Can you imagine AC/DC without electric guitars? Or Def Leppard without their drummer? What if Billy Idol had no Rebel Yell?

Pricing also has three basic components. They are:

- ☆ Time
- ☆ Expenses
- ☆ Profit (of course!)

Over the past seven chapters you have been creating the building blocks for a profitable price. Now it's time to bring them all together.

That's Not Music!

When Elvis first hit the national stage many people declared "That's not music!" When Metallica and Judas Priest popularized hard rock, a chorus of "That's not music!" could be heard again. What they really meant was "That's not good music (in my opinion)."

Even the loudest critics of heavy metal music would grudgingly admit that yes there's singing (of a sort), yes there are instruments (which screech loudly) and yes there's a drummer (flailing wildly in the background). No one picks up an apple and declares "This is music".

Pricing is a combination of art and science. There are basic building blocks in creating a price, just like there are basic ingredients for a rock band. There's not only one answer, just like there's not only one type of music.

This can be very frustrating to entrepreneurs. My clients often tell me to just give them THE answer, or THE solution. Unfortunately that is not the path to success. Just like a musician will never reach superstar status imitating others, business owners must tailor their pricing to their products and services.

Or you can be stuck in the pricing equivalent of a Karaoke bar. UGH.

Time After Time

We've discussed the value of your time. We've discussed the fact that time is an asset. Now we are going to discuss how to ensure you get paid what you're worth.

While Rock Stars may intuitively know their value (or heck just make it up!), in business you need to have a clear understanding to ensure profitability.

In Chapter 3 we calculated the minimum amount you need to pay yourself per hour.

In our example the number was $100, which is what we will use here.

For each of your products or services, you must determine how much time it takes for you to produce or deliver it. Start with your top selling product and work your way down the list.

On the next page is a pricing worksheet for you to use. We'll walk through how to set each number, and calculate a baseline price.

Today we're going to price the Superstar Widget, a must have for every aspiring Rock Star.

Time Assumptions

- ☆ Two hours to create
- ☆ Minimum hourly rate of $100
- ☆ Total cost of time is $200 (2 hours * $100 per hour)

TIME		
a. Number of hours per product created or service provided		2 hours
b. Minimum hourly rate		$100 / hour
c. Total Cost of Time (a * b) =		$200

Pricing Principles 85

PRICING FOR: _____

NUMBER OF SALES PROJECTED: _____

TIME

a. Number of hours per product created or service provided _____

b. Minimum hourly rate _____

c. Total Cost of Time (a * b) = _____

PROFIT

d. Target Profit Goal = _____

EXPENSES

e. Fixed Expenses _____

f. Variable Expenses by Revenue _____

g. Variable Expenses by Sale _____

h. Step Up Expense _____

i. Step Expense Trigger _____

j. Calculate Step Expense _____

Minimum Price Formula: $(c + e + g + j) / (1 - d - f)$

(____ + ____ + ____ + ____) / (1 - ____ - ____)

MINIMUM PRICE: _____

www.FinanceRockStar.com

Set Your Profit Goals

It's time to tackle the second member in our rock group, profit margin. Wondering why we need to include profit? Aren't we already paying ourselves a good wage?

Yes BUT...

- ✯ What if someday you want to pay someone else to create the product or deliver the service? How will you make money?
- ✯ Pricing is not an exact science. A reasonable profit margin also acts as a buffer.
- ✯ You're building a company, not just creating a job for yourself. **Companies make a profit, and yours should too.**

While each person needs to set their own profit margin, I recommend an initial goal of 10%. Absolute minimum would be 5%. When you set a profit goal of 10%, you expect that for every dollar of revenue you bring in, there will be profit of $0.10.

Want to check out your competition? BizStats.com offers this information absolutely free.

Divas Don't Come Cheap

Divas don't come cheap and neither should you. Can you imagine Mariah Carey, Madonna or Barbara Streisand telling their tour promoter "Don't worry about paying for my champagne, my chewing gum disposal attendant (Mariah), the 25 cases of Kabbalah water (Madonna) or the rose petals in the toilet (Babs)"?

Pricing Principles   87

Bottom line, you must cover your expenses!

In Chapter 7 we reviewed your business expense experience, and predicted expenses for the coming year. In the following example we will assume our results from that analysis were:

- ☆ Total Fixed Expenses:
  $15,000
- ☆ Variable Expenses, based on Revenues:
  20% of revenue
- ☆ Variable Expenses, based on Product Sold:
  $30 per Superstar Widget Sold
- ☆ Step Expense:
  $750
- ☆ Step Expense Trigger:
  200 sales

It's time to fill in the *Expenses* portion of the worksheet. In order to fill in this section we need to forecast our sales. For example, the amount for Fixed Expenses listed above ($15,000) is for the entire company. However we need the amount of fixed expenses allocated to a single sale of a single product to fill in item e below. That requires us to forecast sales.

EXPENSES	
e. Fixed Expenses	_____
f. Variable Expenses by Revenue	_____
g. Variable Expenses by Sale	_____
h. Step Up Expense	_____
i. Step Expense Trigger	_____
j. Calculate Step Expense	_____

Sold out Crowd or Empty Seats?

You can get nosebleed tickets to most concerts for under $100. Since they are literally selling tens of thousands of seats, they can sell them at a relatively low price and still meet their profit goals.

What if you wanted your favorite musician or group to perform privately for you or at your event? Be prepared to shell out *seven million dollars* (yes I said million!) if you want the Rolling Stones. You can book Celine Dion for $6.5 million. For bargain shoppers there's Christina Aguilera at $3.6 million.

Realistically predicting your sales volume is crucial.

In setting your price you must consider how many products or services you'll realistically be able to sell. This number can represent your product, services or even hours billed. The key word here is *realistic*.

What if I said I plan to accomplish world peace next year? That's a great goal, but what are my chances of success? Zero is being polite.

- ☆ **Established businesses**
  Look at your sales records from past years. While it's fine to assume some growth, unless you're doubling your sales team don't assume your sales will double.

- ☆ **Young businesses**
  Consider both your sales experience to date and your long term goals. Have you been successful in growing your business by 25%, 50% or more? What are the sales volumes of your established competitors?

- ☆ **Start-ups**
  Start-ups are the toughest. You have no experience and it will take time to build up your client base. In addition, you can't charge the

Rolling Stones Private Event Fee (Mick Jagger you ain't) to the few clients you do bring on in the beginning. Estimate what a reasonable volume may be in two to three years. Do some research into the sales volume of comparable businesses.

For this analysis we are going to assume that last year we sold 140 Superstar Widgets and this year we will sell 150 Superstar Widgets.

Calculating Fixed Expenses for each Superstar Widget Sold.

Most companies sell more than one product or service. *It's important to spread your fixed expenses over all of the products and services you sell.*

In our example we will assume there are ten core products offered. On the right you have been provided an easy worksheet to assist in calculating fixed expense allocations.

Allocating Fixed Expenses

Product Name _____

a. Total Fixed Expenses _____

b. Number of Products or Services You Sell _____

c. Projected Sales for this Product _____

Allocated Expense Formula: a ÷ b ÷ c

Fixed Expenses Per Sale _____

We know our total fixed expenses for the year are $15,000 (a). We sell ten different types of products and services (b). What about sales?

This is where our volume predictions become critical to our profitability. To determine how much we assign to each product sold we divide the allocated fixed expenses by our projected sales numbers (c). In this example our calculation is ($15,000 ÷ 10 ÷ 150) = $10 Fixed Expenses allocated to each Superstar Widget Sold.

> **Underestimating Expenses WILL Cost You Money**
>
> What if we only sell 75 Super Star Widgets?
>
> Our fixed expenses per sale would be $20.
> *($1,500 Fixed Expenses ÷ 75 Sales = $20)*
>
> That means our product is underpriced by $10!
>
> Since we sold 75 Super Star Widgets **we lost $750!**
> *(75 Products * $10 Loss Per Product)*

Calculating Step Expenses for each Superstar Widget Sold.

As discussed in Chapter 7, step expenses are like pizza for a party. Once we hit a certain threshold, if we don't order more pizza someone will go hungry. In our example one "pizza" is $750. One pizza will feed 200 Superstar Widgets.

We've predicted sales of 150. That is well under our 200 limit, so we assume total step expenses of $750. The per product step expense is $50.

$750 Step Expenses ÷ 150 Products Sold = $50 Step Expenses Per Sale

We now have all the information we need to fill in the *Expenses* section.

EXPENSES		
	e. Fixed Expenses	$10
	f. Variable Expenses by Revenue	20%
	g. Variable Expenses by Sale	$30
	h. Step Up Expense	$750
	i. Step Expense Trigger	Every 200 Sales
	j. Calculate Step Expense	$50

Pricing Principles

It's (finally!) time to calculate your price.

All the details of our example are filled in on the opposite page to illustrate the process from soup to nuts.

$$\frac{\text{(Cost of Your Time + Fixed Expense + Per Product Variable Expenses + Step Expense)}}{\text{(1 − Profit Goal − Variable Expenses by Revenue)}}$$

Plugging in our numbers, we get the following equation.

$$\frac{(\$200 + \$10 + \$30 + \$50)}{(1 - 0.10 - 0.20)}$$

Minimum Price: $414.29

You can charge more than the results this process reduces if you believe the market will bear it. Perhaps you offer a unique process, or have strong brand recognition. This number should not limit you, it's only to provide a floor to your price.

Beware: Charging less will cause you to miss your profit goals.

PRICING FOR: _Superstar Widget_

NUMBER OF SALES PROJECTED: _150_

TIME

a. Number of hours per product created or service provided — _2 hours_

b. Minimum hourly rate — _$100 / hour_

c. Total Cost of Time (a * b) = _$200_

PROFIT

d. Target Profit Goal = _10%_

EXPENSES

e. Fixed Expenses — _$10_

f. Variable Expenses by Revenue — _20%_

g. Variable Expenses by Sale — _$30_

h. Step Up Expense — _$750_

i. Step Expense Trigger — _Every 200 Sales_

j. Calculate Step Expense — _$50_

Minimum Price Formula: $(c + e + g + j) / (1 - d - f)$

$(\underline{200} + \underline{10} + \underline{30} + \underline{50}) / (1 - \underline{0.10} - \underline{0.20})$

MINIMUM PRICE: $ _414.29_

www.FinanceRockStar.com

It's Tricky

Remember I said that Step Expenses were tricky?

As discussed in Chapter 7, step expenses are like the pizza for our party. Once we hit a certain threshold, if we don't order more pizza someone will go hungry. *In our business, once we hit a certain threshold, if we don't bump up people or capacity a client will not receive top quality services or timely delivery of goods.*

While I would love to say all finance is cut and dry, the reality is that pricing can be more art than science. Here are a few examples to illustrate where the art, or judgment factor, comes into play.

Art vs. Science: Example 1

We expect to sell 220 products. In our example we project the need to step up when we sell 200 products in a year. Should we step up?

- ☆ We expect to exceed our step up threshold by 20 products, or 10% (20/200) which is a large margin.
- ☆ Step up!

Art vs. Science: Example 2

We expect to sell 201 products. In our example we project the need to step up when we sell 200 products in a year. Should we step up?

It depends (oh yes I did!). Really it does.

- ☆ *Scenario A*
  You believe that hitting 201 in sales this year is a long shot, and it's extremely unlikely you'll surpass it. In this case I would recommend NOT stepping up the expenses.

☆ *Scenario B*
You know that you're already stretching your resources to the max in waiting until 200 products to step up this expense. Given this information I would recommend stepping up, since you may even need the resources sooner than the 200 mark.

☆ *Scenario C*
You set your step up benchmark conservatively low. You probably won't need to step up until about 225 products. If you truly think the estimate was overly conservative, then I would recommend NOT stepping up the expense.

Art vs. Science: Example 3

What if you expect an absolutely banner sales year? You've got a great new campaign, awesome innovative services, and you believe you'll absolutely hit your sales out of the park?

- ☆ You plan to move 700 Superstar Widgets.
- ☆ Clearly you'll need to add resources. The question is how much?
- ☆ Since we expect such a high growth rate, we need to consider stepping up our expenses more significantly. Simply divide the total sales number by your Step Expenses Factor (700 ÷ 200 = 3.5). *You'll need to step up twice, or add $1,500 in expenses.*

Rock Stars Don't Own Geese

I'm sure you've heard the parable of the goose that laid golden eggs. I often come across entrepreneurs online who think that such a goose exists. EBooks, eCourses, affiliate programs – set and forget income opportunities. Unfortunately they are all as mythical as the goose.

Let's take a common example, writing and then selling an eBook. This is a common way to earn money online, and if you're simply selling it yourself, relatively low-cost and low time requirements.

Many entrepreneurs assume that they can simply write the eBook, create a sales page, add an affiliate program and the profits will simply start rolling in. It's like printing money!

Hold on. When was the last time you purchased a business book written five years ago? Heck even 5 months ago? This is a NOW society.

That doesn't even factor in the fact that you need to nurture, maintain and motivate your affiliates. Planning to sell everything yourself? Have you considered how you will stand out from the other billions of pages online?

There's no product or service you can create that will magically generate unending profit without additional work. Therefore you must plan how you spend your time to leverage your income.

CHAPTER NINE
Pricing Multiple Products

Today's Rock Stars are kings (and queens) of leveraging their brand and their fan base into multiple sources of income. Of course they make money by selling their albums and performing concerts. Both at live events and online these masters of merchandising sell T-Shirts, hats and other clothing.

Taking it a step further, artists will pursue sponsors (as we discussed in Chapter Four). Some even license their music for commercials. From Madonna to Eminem this can be seen on TV and online.

Once you have priced each product or service individually, it is crucial to do an overall company review to ensure that your business is on track to deliver your profit goals.

Come As You Are

In the early 90's grunge band Nirvana made a huge splash promoting non-comformity and individuality. You must recognize that your core products are unique, requiring different amounts of time, expenses and potentially even profit levels. A word of caution - don't go overboard on having too many different options. Moderation is key.

Pricing Your Suite of Products

I recommend my coaching clients start with their top ten core products or services. Often they discover any remaining offerings are either underperforming or simply a minor variation on the top ten.

Be realistic with your expenses, time and profit expectations. Often businesses discover that some offerings have a lower margin to remain competitive and others can provide a higher profit margin. *This can work for your business overall as long as none of your products actually lose money.*

Revisit Chapter 8, and tackle your top ten products now.

The Big Picture

Most businesses sell a range of products. Often there's a low priced offering, which I like to call the gateway product. It gives new customers a chance to try you out without risking a lot of money.

Consider musicians today. Most sell a single song on iTunes for one dollar. That's their gateway offering. If you like the song you'll download more, perhaps buy a T-shirt. Next time they come to your town you may attend their concert, even spring for backstage passes. You can see how the purchase size grows over time, and it all started with a single song.

While reviewing your overall product portfolio, be sure to consider if you offer a range of price points to your target market. **Keep in mind all your products must be profitable.** Even at one dollar per song, I can guarantee you that musicians are not losing money.

An easy total company product worksheet has been included on the next page. While at first blush it may be intimidating notice that you've already determined most of the numbers to fill in. The few calculations required are straightforward. *You could even do them on a dollar store calculator.*

Why do this? If each product is profitable why do we need yet another worksheet? What if I said I've got a great guitarist, a drummer who can get the crowd rocking and a singer with an out of this world voice *but they're each playing a different song.* Do you think the final show would be any good?

The products and services offered by your company don't operate in a vacuum. They need to be working together, or you'll end up with a mess like my poorly coordinated rock group discussed in the previous paragraph.

Here are the specific sources for the product portfolio analysis:

- ☆ **Product Column**
  Fill in the name of your product.

- ☆ **Price**
  Use the price we determined in the previous chapter. It can be higher than our result, but not lower.

- ☆ **Flat Expenses Per Product**
  Refer back to the pricing worksheet from the previous chapter. Add together your results for Fixed Expenses (e), Variable Expenses by Sale (g) and Step Expenses (j). In the example provided the answer is $90 ($10 + $30 + $50).

- ☆ **Variable Expenses**
  In the pricing worksheet from Chapter 8 use line (f), Variable Expenses by Revenue.

Product	Price (a)	Flat Expenses Per Product (b)	Variable Expenses (c)	Profit Margin (d)	Projected Sales (e)	CALCULATIONS			
						Total Revenue (f) (a * e)	Total Flat Expenses (b * e)	Total Variable Expenses (c * f)	Total Profit (d * f)
TOTALS									

www.FinanceRockStar.com

- ☆ **Profit Margin**
  This must match number used in pricing the product, line (d). If you don't use a positive number for your profit margin you will lose money every time you sell something. *You will be paying people to use your service or take your product if this number is less than zero.*

- ☆ **Expected Sales**
  On the top of the individual product pricing worksheet you included your projected sales. This projection must be consistently used or your analysis will not make sense.

Worksheet calculation instructions – it's easy, Scout's Honor!

- ☆ **Total Revenue (Column f)**
  Price (a) x Projected Sales (e)

- ☆ **Total Flat Expenses**
  Flat Expenses Per Product (b) x Projected Sales (e)

- ☆ **Total Variable Expenses**
  Variable Expenses (c) x Total Revenue (f)

- ☆ **Total Profit**
  Profit Margin (d) x Total Revenue (f)

- ☆ **Total Company Profit Margin**
  This is an extremely important number to calculate, particularly if some of your products were priced with margins below your overall target. Simply divide the total from the profits column by the total from the revenue column.

  In this example, $12,000 ÷ $114,750 = 10.5%

Pricing Multiple Products

Product	Price (a)	Flat Expenses Per Product (b)	Variable Expenses (c)	Profit Margin (d)	Projected Sales (e)	CALCULATIONS			
						Total Revenue (f) (a * e)	Total Flat Expenses (b * e)	Total Variable Expenses (c * f)	Total Profit (d * f)
Super Star Widget	$415	$90	20%	10%	150	$62,250	$13,500	$12,450	$6,225
Elvis Makeover	$300	$70	20%	14%	100	$30,000	$7,000	$6,000	$4,200
Grunge Goodies	$100	$55	20%	7%	225	$22,500	$12,375	$4,500	$1,575
TOTALS				10.5%	475	$114,750	$32,875	$22,950	$12,000

www.FinanceRockStar.com

Don't be a ~~Freddie~~ Freeloader

Once you've completed this exercise it's time to verify all expenses have been allocated. Don't worry this is really easy! Add up the two columns of expenses from the worksheet and compare to your budget. In this example you would add $32, 875 + $22,950 for a total of $55,825.

If the number from your pricing worksheet is lower than your actual budget, you have a freeloader! You need to revisit and increase expense assumptions.

If the total expenses from your pricing worksheet are the same or higher than your actual budget you have covered everything.

As discussed previously, some products may require a lower profit margin to remain competitive. If you use this strategy then other products must have a higher than target profit margin to even things out. Use the worksheet to calculate your total company expected profit margin. If it is less than your goal you need to make changes.

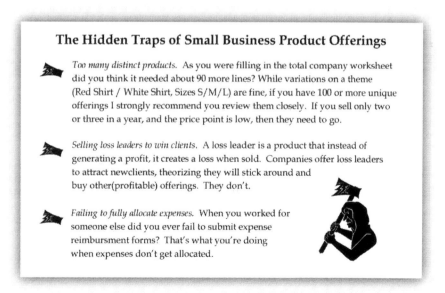

The Hidden Traps of Small Business Product Offerings

- *Too many distinct products.* As you were filling in the total company worksheet did you think it needed about 90 more lines? While variations on a theme (Red Shirt / White Shirt, Sizes S/M/L) are fine, if you have 100 or more unique offerings I strongly recommend you review them closely. If you sell only two or three in a year, and the price point is low, then they need to go.

- *Selling loss leaders to win clients.* A loss leader is a product that instead of generating a profit, it creates a loss when sold. Companies offer loss leaders to attract newclients, theorizing they will stick around and buy other(profitable) offerings. They don't.

- *Failing to fully allocate expenses.* When you worked for someone else did you ever fail to submit expense reimbursment forms? That's what you're doing when expenses don't get allocated.

Pricing Multiple Products

CHAPTER TEN
Discounts, Promotions and Sales

Find out how much sales really cost you!

Everyone loves a sale, special offer, or promotion right?

It generates interest, traffic, unloads old stock or fills up empty hours. What's not to love? Not so fast! Have you priced for it?

Do you really think that all those big box stores who routinely offer 40% off sales don't include that in their pricing? At the beginning of the year they assume a certain amount of their products or services will sell at a discount. (It doesn't matter which type of sale, 40% off, BOGO, or store credit if you spend so much).

These promotions are reflected in their regular prices.

If you want to offer specials, incentives or any type of discount during the year you must plan for it now. *Otherwise that offer is coming right out of your pocket.*

If you don't plan for specials and promotions now, it's like writing a check to your clients out of your personal bank account. Why not throw a grenade into your profits now?

Here are quick and easy solutions to leave room for promotions and sales.

Pump up the ~~Volume~~ Prices

The quickest option to cover sales and promotions is a flat price bump for all products and services. It's so easy, I bet you can get it done in five minutes and have time left to spare!

☆ Estimate the amount of products you plan to sell at a discount. For our example we will assume 20% of products to be sold at a discounted price.

☆ Estimate the average discount you'll offer. For our example we assume the average customer discount to be 30%.

☆ Multiply the percentage you expect to sell at a discount times the average customer discount. 20% * 30% = 6%.

☆ *You must increase all prices by this amount.* New Price Formula: Current Price ÷ (1 − Percentage Increase). If we assume the current price is $100, the new price is $100 ÷ (1-0.06) = $106.38.

Haven't I Seen You Before?

I'm sure you've heard the mantra that it's cheaper to keep a current client than find a new one. It's absolutely true and opens up profitable ways to reward loyal customers.

Consider what costs you only incur for new business. Perhaps it's a commission, or maybe it's an investment of your time to sell your services. Only consider expenses that you'll not have for repeat customers.

Max's No Bull Corner

Common New Client Expenses
- ❏ Commissions
- ❏ Marketing
- ❏ Administrative Set-up
- ❏ Your time to find and win the client

Now spend this money on your returning clients, preferably the VIP ones. For example, if you determine it costs you an extra $200 to win a new account, offer a service or benefit worth $200 to a valued existing customer.

Use Your Marketing Budget

It sounds odd, odder than Acid Jazz (yes that is a sub-genre of music), but it's a great way to keep your budget on track.

Let's say you have a marketing budget of $5,000 which you plan to spend on traditional advertising, PPC and targeted Banner Ads.

You've decided to run a sale, and it's a huge success bringing in $8,000 in revenue. If the products had been sold at regular price you would have generated $9,000 in revenue.

Your clients saved $1,000, which is great for them. What about you? If you do nothing, it will come out of your pocket. Not good.

The answer is simple. Count it as part of your marketing budget. Instead of spending $5,000 on advertising this year, reduce the amount to $4,000. The remaining $1,000 has been "spent" on your sale keeping your profits whole.

To achieve your profit goals while offering sales or promotions you *must* account for all lost revenue.

SECTION FOUR
Hitting the Stage

The stage is set, the stadium is full, and the band is ready. It's time to take this show live!

Running a business, even with a carefully crafted plan, is a risk. **The key to success is stacking the odds in your favor.** The first chapter in this section introduces you to a simple, yet effective tool to manage your risk and resources while pursuing your profit goals.

Then it's time to set your Key Metrics. **Learn how to create a business scoreboard that reports on your performance in a glance**. Business is a competition, and you want to win.

Rock Stars travel with a whole smorgasbord of people. They have stage managers, roadies, grips, lighting experts, sound techs and more. As awesome as you are, you too need help for some things in your business. **This chapter covers when to get help and how to find it.**

Understand how to track progress and make needed course corrections. Even superstars make mistakes. **Learn how to bounce back and be more successful than ever.**

CHAPTER ELEVEN
Viva Las Vegas

Love it or hate it, Las Vegas can teach every entrepreneur about investing money. Sounds ridiculous, doesn't it? Especially coming from someone whose idea of going crazy at a casino is playing the $3 craps table until my $20 is gone.

The reality is that all entrepreneurs and small business owners are gamblers. **We just know how to stack the odds in our favor.**

Once you embrace this concept, a simple, effective tool is at your fingertips.

Las Vegas has always been closely associated with big musical acts. In the 60's there was the Rat Pack; Frank, Dean, Sammy and Joey.

Then came Elvis, who never really left. Now there's Cher and Celine Dion. What better place to have the (imaginary) Finance Rock Star Casino?

In its broadest definition, gambling is betting money on uncertain events. No one can be 100% certain they will succeed (okay, at this point, Oprah is unlikely to fail), but you CAN rig this game. For the first, last and only time, I'm going to recommend you don't play fair.

I will walk you through a simple exercise to stack the odds of business success in your favor. This easy and versatile tool will amaze you.

Get Ready

While I have created a ready-made budgeting kit for entrepreneurs, this exercise can be done with some paper, Post It notes, a pen, and either loose change or poker chips.

You don't need to be an artist or a finance expert to use this technique!

We are going to use a marketing budget for this example. Your budget for the year is $10,000. This includes a Trade Show, Online Pay Per Click (PPC) Ads and Traditional Media Ads.

Start with the basics:

- ☆ *Budget you're analyzing:* Marketing
- ☆ *Amount of money allocated to this budget:* $10,000
- ☆ *Amount of time allocated to this budget*:* 240 hours
- ☆ *Main budget categories:* Trade Show, PPC Ads, Traditional Media

*As discussed in Chapter 8, **your time IS an asset**, therefore it must be part of the budgeting process. Spend it wisely.

For this exercise we have committed 12% of working hours to Marketing. In Chapter 2 we set our hours and vacation schedule, coming up with

2,000 hours for the year (40 hours per week * 50 weeks per year = 2,000 hours). Time budgeted for Marketing is 240 hours (2,000 hours *12%).

BUDGET FOR: _____
BUDGETED AMOUNT: $ _____
BUDGETED TIME: _____

Cost:
Profit:
ROI:
Risk:

Cost:
Profit:
ROI:
Risk:

Cost:
Profit:
ROI:
Risk:

Cost:
Profit:
ROI:
Risk:

www.FinanceRockStar.com

Box 1: Trade Show Analysis

Assumptions

- ✯ Cost to attend is $2,500. This includes travel, additional marketing materials required, booth fee and so forth.
- ✯ Expected Net Profit is $9,500.

Calculating Return on Investment

As we covered in Chapter 7, ROI (Return on Investment) provides a great way to compare the benefits of different opportunities. Now it's time to put that knowledge to use.

$$ROI = (Profit - Cost) \div Cost$$

We know that the expected profit is $9,500. You might be tempted to think the cost is just $2,500. Remember time is money, and 40 hours of your time does have value.

In Chapter 3 we calculated a value of $100 for one hour of time. That means the cost of our time for the Trade Show would be 40 * $100 = $4,000. Total cost of the Trade Show is $6,500 = $2,500 + $4,000.

Trade Show ROI = 46%
($9,500 Profit − $6,500 Cost) ÷ $6,500 Cost

Assessing Risk

The Trade Show is a new marketing channel. You have never attended one before, and have no past experience. Plus you only have one shot to do it right. *If you bomb at the Trade Show you're out of luck.*

Therefore, the risk level is High.

Trade Show

Cost: $2,500 & 40 hours
Profit: $9,500
ROI: 46%
Risk: HIGH

Box 2: Pay Per Click (PPC) Ads Analysis

While the Trade Show is a one-time investment, PPC ads can be purchased in units. Most importantly, they can also be turned off or ramped up depending on the results achieved.

Assumptions

- ☆ Cost per unit of PPC Ads is $100.
- ☆ Expected net profit per unit of PPC Ads is $625.

Calculating Return on Investment

$$ROI = (Profit - Cost) \div Cost$$

Again, we need to include the cost of our time. In Chapter 3 we calculated a value of $100 for one hour of time. Therefore the cost of our time for the PPC Ads would be 4 hours * $100 per hour = $400. Total cost of the PPC Ads is $500 = $100 + $400.

PPC Ads ROI = 25%
($625 Profit − $500 Cost) ÷ $500 Cost

Assessing Risk

You have limited experience with PPC Ads. While the returns to date have been strong, you need more proof that you can expect the results consistently. Since these are purchased in units, it allows you to stop if profits fall off a cliff. The capability to limit losses reduces the overall risk.

Therefore, the risk level is Medium.

> PPC Ads
> Cost: $100 & 4 hours / unit
> Profit: $625
> ROI: 25%
> Risk: MEDIUM

Box3: Traditional Media Ads Analysis

As with the PPC Ads, Traditional Media ads can be purchased in units. They can be turned off or ramped up depending on the results achieved

Assumptions

- ☆ Cost per unit of Traditional Media Ad is $500.
- ☆ Expected net profit per unit of Traditional Media Ads is $1,210.

Calculating Return on Investment

$$ROI = (Profit - Cost) \div Cost$$

Again, we need to include the cost of our time. In Chapter 3 we calculated a value of $100 for one hour of time. Therefore the cost of our time for the Traditional Media Ads would be 6 hours * $100 per hour = $600. Total cost of the Traditional Media Ads is $500 = $600 + $1,100.

Traditional Media Ads ROI = 10%
($1,210 Profit − $1,100 Cost) ÷ $1,100 Cost

Assessing Risk

Your company has a great deal of experience with Traditional Ads. They have consistently delivered their expected return. In addition, they can be purchased in relatively small units, providing the option to stop or redirect if they unexpectedly fail to perform.

Therefore, the risk level is Low.

Traditional Media

Cost: *$500 & 6 hours / unit*
Profit: *$1,210*
ROI: *10%*
Risk: *Low*

Box4: Unplanned Opportunities and Mad Scientist Experiments

Every business owner has come across a truly compelling, unexpected opportunity. An opportunity that was not in the budget. While I would never recommend blindly jumping at every "sure thing" you see, you can plan for a bit of experimentation.

Smart entrepreneurs have a cushion or the marketing equivalent of fun money, worked into their budget. You never know when a fantastic, unplanned, opportunity will land in your lap. Or you may get struck by mad-scientist-like inspiration that must be tested.

Just remember, all the ideas your fevered brain imagines at 2 a.m. do not need to see the light of day. Meat dress ~~Lady Gaga~~ anyone?

The Gambler

Do you know why casinos don't place the odds at the Roulette Wheel, Craps Table or Poker Table? **The odds favor the casino, not you.**

Casinos won't change their policies anytime soon, but you can *lay out your business odds clearly.* You'll know the allocation of your budget, the expected return and the risk at a glance!

Why is the risk component so important? If the odds of a 50% return are only 5%, do you really think that is the best place to put your whole marketing budget? This keeps you from betting wildly or recklessly.

Ready to place your bets?

When placing your bets, be sure to limit your chips to the value of your budget. In this example, we have a total of 240 hours to allocate. That is the equivalent of 6, 40-hour chips. As you can see, they have been placed on the different initiatives and there are an additional 40 remaining for any unplanned opportunities.

1 Chip = 40 hours
Total Chips = 6
Value of Chips = 240 hours

1 Chip = $500
Total Chips = 2
Value of Chips = $1,000

1 Chip = $1,000
Total Chips = 4
Value of Chips = $4,000

1 Chip = $5,000
Total Chips = 1
Value of Chips = $5,000

BUDGET FOR: _Marketing_
BUDGETED AMOUNT: $ _10,000_
BUDGETED TIME: _240 Hours_

Trade Show
Cost: $2,500 & 40 hours
Profit: $9,500
ROI: 46%
Risk: HIGH

PPC Ads
Cost: $100 & 4 hours / unit
Profit: $625
ROI: 25%
Risk: MEDIUM

Traditional Media
Cost: $500 & 6 hours / unit
Profit: $1,210
ROI: 10%
Risk: LOW

Unplanned Opportunities
Cost:
Profit:
ROI:
Risk:

www.FinanceRockStar.com

Luck be a Lady

What does this accomplish?

- ☆ On one page you can review where your money is going, what you expect it to accomplish, and how much risk you're taking

- ☆ This exercise ensures you budget time *and* money. Add up the time allocated for each budget category (marketing, sales, administration, etc) and compare it to your annual plan. In this example we set out a total of 2,000 hours. If you add everything up and get 3,000 that is a huge red flag!

- ☆ We will use this information in Chapter 13 to set key metrics.

Common Questions

This seems like a lot of work. Does it really add value?

Just like in a casino, it's easy to get carried away. Think of the excitement around a winning craps table, or the screams when someone wins big at the slots or roulette wheel.

Doesn't part of you just itch to join in? That's what the casinos want. And that emotion is what marketing materials and sales people strive to evoke. That's not right or wrong, it just is.

This one page overview is your antidote to the Buy, Buy, Buy hysteria.

How do you calculate return on administrative tasks?

You don't. Unfortunately, there are some expenses that are the cost of doing business, and can't be expected to generate profits or a return. Examples include filing your taxes, managing your books, and contract review to name a few.

When you create a budgeting page for administrative expenses simply leave ROI blank or (my preference) put in CODB (Cost of Doing Business). Remember you must allocate time for these activities.

What if my total budgeted hours are 50% more than I plan to work?

It means the goals you have set cannot be realistically accomplished in the hours you have. When I'm faced with this I look to see if I've missed any possible efficiencies in my business. If you can't find any, you must either scale back your goals or bring in more resources.

Will this help me in my day to day life?

Absolutely! This exercise instills discipline. Leave it out on your desk or tacked on your wall as a constant visual reminder of your assets and how you plan to use them to achieve your goals.

Save now on budgeting tools that won't bore you to tears.

CHAPTER TWELVE
We Will Rock You!

It's time to hit the stage and Rock Your Profits!

Releasing your business plan into the wild is like a Rock Star going on stage to perform. *Good live acts don't just get up on stage and hope for the best.* They have earpieces for sound checks, visual cues with the other band members, and even ways to signal to the lighting and effects people when there's a problem.

When big names go on tour they use the opening act to warm up the crowd and work out any bugs in the system before they take the stage. While fans may be forgiving of the up-and-coming talent, they expect a professional show from the headliner.

You need ways to determine if your show (business plan) is going well once it's live. If you wait until the end to discover the lights weren't working, or the vocals couldn't be heard, the audience will not be happy. They will certainly tell others it stunk, they may never pay to see you again, and there's even a possibility they'll even demand their money back!

How do you keep things running smoothly once you're live?

- ✩ Set Your Key Metrics
- ✩ Track Your Key Metrics
- ✩ Fix Your Problems Fast

Setting Key Metrics

When musicians get on stage they don't worry about every little detail. If someone misses a chord, or steps in the wrong spot once, it's no big deal. The audience probably won't even know and certainly will not remember.

However there are some problems which will kill a show. All the stage lights go out. The speaker system dies or gets stuck in one of those head exploding feedback loops. You may not be able to prevent a problem, but like the best live rock bands, you must be ready to fix it.

You need to outline the show stoppers for your business and KISS.

Not KISS the band. Although they certainly knew how to rock a live concert for their fans, I'm talking about the **Keep It Simple Stupid (KISS) rule**.

You're probably expecting this numbers geek to declare a list of 50 (or even 100!) things you absolutely have to look at every single month. Fear not. That would be breaking the KISS rule. No one has time to do that.

Here are some quick and easy ideas for your monthly business metrics.

Total Revenue

- ✩ In Chapter 9 we calculated the revenue for all of our products and services. In the example on page 102 we had three products, with a total of $114,750 in revenue.

✩ The simplest way to set your monthly revenue metric is to divide the total by 12. That would give you projected revenues of $9,562 for each month to hit your plan ($114,750 ÷ 12 months = $9,562).

✩ However in most businesses that is not realistic. For example in retail you should plan to be heavily weighted to the 4th quarter. For a business that has courses or launches, the upticks should reflect when you'll be enrolling or launching something new.

✩ Don't overthink this. The numbers are simply meant to be a best guess and a general benchmark, not tattooed on your forehead.

✩ The grid below can be used for both your historical analysis and your projections. It's important to consider why you have dips or spikes in experience. What if your sales were huge in March of last year because you had a big promotion? To expect those results again you need to plan another promotion.

Month	Revenues	Events or Factors
January		
February		
March		
April		
May		
June		
July		
August		
September		
October		
November		
December		

Total Sales

✩ Back in Chapter 9 we also calculated our total projected sales. Your metric might have been number of products, services or even billable hours. In the example we predicted total sales of 475.

✩ *The number of sales per month should have the same distribution as revenues.* If you simply divided by 12, then your answer here would be 39.58 (feel free to round up to 40!). If you believe the number should be higher in the 4th quarter do that here as well.

✩ Repeat business versus new customers is also something to consider. **Maintaining your current client base while attracting new clients is an important balancing act.** Your current clients provide the foundation, and the new business drives your growth, ignoring either one can jeopardize your profits.

Month	Number of Sales	Percentage of New Client Sales
January		
February		
March		
April		
May		
June		
July		
August		
September		
October		
November		
December		

Total Expenses

☆ You've already calculated all your per product expenses (whew!) in Chapter 9. From our example we expect $55,825 in total expenses ($32,875 + $22,950). If evenly distributed across all twelve months, we would expect our monthly expenses to be $4,652.08.

☆ As with the first two metrics, review your past experience. If you know that there's a big annual expense in May, then reflect it. Otherwise use the same distribution as revenues and sales.

Month	Expenses	Events or Factors
January		
February		
March		
April		
May		
June		
July		
August		
September		
October		
November		
December		

Watch Out - Expenses Can Eat Your ~~Lunch~~ Profit

Ignorance is not bliss when dealing with expenses. Don't give into the temptation to skip them as a Key Metric! All the revenue in the world won't matter if your expenses are out of control.

Other Possible Metrics

All businesses were not created equal. Some sell services, others widgets. Some sell to consumers, others to corporations or even governments! Consider what are one or two other activities or metrics that are crucial to your continued success. **Only use metrics that are measurable and objective.**

For example you may look at your sales funnel conversion rate. If you do a lot of business with net payment terms (meaning the client pays after you have provided the product or service) consider adding your Accounts Receivables balance. You may decide that the percentage of new clients versus existing clients is important enough to include as a key metric.

Your Key Metrics at a Glance

Month	Revenues	# Sales	Expenses	*Optional* 4th *Metric*	*Optional* 5th *Metric*
January					
February					
March					
April					
May					
June					
July					
August					
September					
October					
November					
December					

Track Your Key Metrics

Print out your key metrics for the current month and post in a place you'll see it every day. Or write it on the most visible white board in your office. This will help you, and your employees, focus on the things that are most important every day.

As soon as possible after the month ends, tabulate your actual results for each of the key metrics. Let's say the month ended, and you determined you had the following experience:

- ☆ $10,500 in Revenue
- ☆ 52 New Product Sales
- ☆ $2,500 of Expenses

In this scenario you exceeded your revenue target, beat your new sales goal and had lower expenses than budgeted. That's great! Your show is on track to be a blockbuster, there are no major problems to address today.

What if your revenues only came in at $8,000 or your expenses topped $3,000? Then you know something is wrong, and it's time to...

Fix Your Problems Fast

On tour Rock Stars have roadies to work out all the technical glitches. As a small business owner or Solopreneur, you're your own best roadie. So when something has clearly gone wrong you need to jump in, find the problem, and fix it fast before it ruins the show.

Did you have lower than expected revenues? Here are a few common causes and ideas on how to address the problem.

- ☆ *Your marketing campaign failed to deliver as expected*
  Did it start late? Was there a failure to execute the full campaign? If the campaign has been not been fully implemented consider

giving it another month before labeling it a failure. However if the campaign was implemented in full, and the results were disappointing, you need to go back to the drawing board for new ideas, or fall back on proven (but perhaps less glamorous) options.

> ☆ *Your average price was lower than expected.*
> Did you sell a bunch of your gateway product, but little of your higher end offerings? Are you effectively following up with clients once they've made their initial purchase? Consider that you may not have aligned the right product with the right market.

Were your sales numbers lower than expected?

> ☆ *A specific product or service that didn't perform.*
> You may want to consider that the demand for a new product is not as high as you anticipated. Perhaps you overestimated the amount clients would be willing to pay. Consider working on your sales pitch, as well as seeking market feedback.

> ☆ *An underperforming sales channel.*
> Did you expect to get 10% of new business from Google Ads, but ended up with a big donut (zero)? Did you plan to have referrals account for 20%, but so far they are only 5%? Even if a certain channel was amazing last year, it may fall flat this year.

Were your expenses higher than expected? I can't stress enough how important it is to stay on top of your expenses. More times than I care to count I've heard an entrepreneur say, "But my sales were great. Why didn't I make more money?" and the answer is expenses.

> ☆ *There was a large non-recurring expense.*
> If you had the amount in the budget, but spread out over all twelve months this is not a major concern. However future months should be significantly lower.

☆ *There was an increase in the cost of your raw goods.* Did a commodity price jump up, something that you need to produce your product? Perhaps you do a great deal of driving for your work and gas prices went up.

☆ *You had an unplanned expense.*
No matter how well you plan, there are some things that you simply can't anticipate. Your laptop gets stolen. Your widget producing machine breaks down. These things happen. Look for other places in your budget you can cut back to cover the cost.

Champions (and Rock Stars) adapt. You must determine the source of a sub-par performance. If a rock star was worried about the lighting, when the real issue is a major feedback problem, do you think it's going to get fixed?

Once you've got the source attack the problem with all your ingenuity and determination. Your bank account depends on it.

CHAPTER THIRTEEN
(Don't Be) Dancing on Your Own

When bands go on tour they bring a small village. They need people to haul around their instruments, set up the lighting, manage the sound board, construct the stage, run any special effects,... the list is endless.

So why do small business owners, solopreneurs (the worst offenders!) and entrepreneurs believe they must do everything themselves? Would you expect to see Barbara Streisand running around setting up lights? Or Snoop Dog manning the sound board (not to mention hard to do when you're supposed to be singing at the same time).

Musicians that are known for their extravagant live performances know they need to outsource. They do it thoughtfully, hiring the right talent.

Make Me Over

Love them or hate them, makeover shows are part of the American culture. I confess I have a secret addiction to TLC's *What Not to Wear*. Did you ever notice they don't expect the guest to make themselves over?

I'm not saying you need to become a Finance Geek. (*Although if you do I'm happy to send you the super-secret application form in triplicate.*) I'm saying get help with your business. Help can come in a variety of shapes and sizes, and often does not require hiring additional employees.

All you may need is someone to assist you in organizing and understanding your financials. Then you can manage them on your own, with the occasional check-up. Just like a wash and wear haircut.

Uncle Sam

While it's easy to think of the government as a roadblock to success, there are actually a number of great free resources available to you! **Score.org** is a non-profit that works with the SBA, and can provide free assistance with loan applications and business plans.

Visit www.SBA.gov for a complete list of small business resources offered by the government.

Taxman

No one likes to do their taxes, even me. Yes The Numbers Whisperer™ pays someone else to do her taxes. Not *just* because I hate doing them (although that is a good enough reason for me). Taxes take a specialized knowledge, one that I don't have and don't want.

Every year my CPA (Certified Public Accountant) saves me more money than they charge. That's right, their services pay for themselves. Talk about a guilt free indulgence!

You may also consider hiring an Enrolled Agent (EA). These are private individuals who have either passed a three-part comprehensive IRS test covering individual and business tax returns, or have experience as a former IRS agent.

Choosing a Tax Professional

- Get referrals from trusted business associates

- Verify the tax professional has experience with the type of business you run. If you're a freelance artist and they've only worked with plumbers it may not be a good fit

- Does the tax professional have experience with the type of legal structure you use? The states in which you operate? This isn't the place to be a guinea pig!

- Understand their audit policy upfront. Will they provide audit support free of charge? If not, what fees would you incur?

Other Resources

Hire a profit coach (like me!), to work with you on pricing and achieving your profit goals. Join a mastermind group. Review the course offerings of your community college. Find out if your local business associations offer training sessions or continuing education. **Bottom line, there are tons of reasonably priced options out there to help with your Finance Makeover.**

CHAPTER FOURTEEN
Surviving Glitter

Mariah Carey is the ultimate comeback story in current pop music. In 2000 she left her record label, Columbia, and signed a record-breaking $100 million recording contract with Virgin Records. In 2001 Mariah had her first starring role in a film called *Glitter*. Haven't heard of it? I'm not surprised. It tanked at the box office.

That same year Mariah essentially had a nervous breakdown, and went silent for a few years. After a few unsuccessful attempts at reigniting her singing career Mariah hit it big with The Emancipation of Mimi (2005). Its second single "We Belong Together" became the most successful solo single of her music career.

Not content with her singing comeback Mariah tried her hand again at acting. Her role in the movie Precious was well-received and she was awarded the "Breakthrough Performance Award" at the Palm Springs International Film Festival.

I remember when Mariah's career went dark in 2001. I remember her being on the receiving end of many not so nice jokes. *I remember thinking, her career is over.*

Boy was I wrong.

How many times does an entrepreneur fail? Or at least fail to achieve all their stated goals? How many times does an entrepreneur get told, "Your business is dead." Or "Your career is over."?

I'm Not Dead

If you're still breathing, you still have a chance to succeed. *You only fail when you quit trying.* I bet even as Mariah licked her wounds, she was thinking "Don't count me out."

As entrepreneurs we can learn a great deal from her.

Take Care of Yourself First

While we can never be sure exactly what happened, it's clear Mariah was not taking care of herself and had a breakdown. You can't accomplish anything if you're in the hospital, or passed out from exhaustion. **You must give yourself permission to rest.**

In fact, a number of studies now show there's a connection between your physical well-being and your mental acumen. Exercise, even just walking, sharpens your mind. Personally I find **exercise stimulates creative thinking**. Inspiration for a new product, or solution to a current problem, has often struck when I'm running.

While it's tempting to work for "just another 15 minutes", or to "finish one thing" on your day off, you need to **give yourself permission to rest**. I've never heard someone say in the twilight of their life, I wish I would have worked more. Have you?

I *have* heard people say they regret working too much, they regret missing out on their kids' childhood, or that they regret not taking regular vacations. Why did you start your own business in the first place? I often hear small business owners say they wanted more freedom and flexibility in their life and schedule. Yet that seems to be one of the first casualties of entrepreneurship.

There will always be more work to do, but there won't always be more days to enjoy the results of that work.

Return to Your Core Strength

Mariah is, was, and will be a singer first. Love her or hate her, you've got to admit her vocal skills are impressive. Mariah's comeback strategy was smart, she focused first on rejuvenating her musical career.

If you're looking to make a comeback, or overcome a bad decision, return to your core strength with laser focus. Determine which product or service that should serve as your standard bearer. Ensure that product is priced to achieve your profit goals. **Then promote it with single minded determination.**

Sounds simple right? Yet I often see small business owners who are struggling do the exact opposite. They jump on every bandwagon under the sun, hoping *something* will work. This more is better philosophy actually works against them.

First it confuses your potential customers. If they see you selling plumbing fixtures one day, and branding services the next, they will buy neither. Second, it scatters your focus and energy. It would be the equivalent of a musician trying to excel at playing the guitar, the piano, the cello and the trombone. Not going to happen.

Get Back on the Horse

Once her comeback was firmly recognized Mariah tried her hand again at acting. Although it's unlikely she'll ever win an Oscar, she did receive some critical acclaim and finally put to rest the bitter taste of Glitter.

Still think your idea or product can be a hit? You may want to give it another try once you've re-established yourself. **Re-establishing your reputation for your core strength first is absolutely critical.** Without that baseline of credibility it will be virtually impossible.

Imagine if Mariah's first act in her attempt to make a comeback was to audition for a role in the movie *Precious*. Do you think the casting director would want to risk putting the punch line of a joke in his movie? It was her successful comeback as a singer that gave her credibility to pursue acting again. In fact, I believe the casting agent considered Mariah in part because she would attract her stronger than ever fan base.

Be Realistic

Sometimes, no matter how brilliant you think an idea is, there's simply no appetite in the market. Or you may not have the skills to deliver on the idea. **Don't let your ego get in the way of making the right business decision.**

Madonna's acting career is a great example of this. While she had some initial success with *Desperately Seeking Susan,* her later attempts fell flat. It wasn't until the complete failure of *Swept Away* (directed by her then husband), did Madonna seem to accept acting isn't her core strength.

Even incredibly smart, resourceful and successful people can have ideas or products that don't succeed. Even incredibly smart, resourceful and talented people can't succeed at everything. I'd love to be a singer, but my voice wouldn't get me past the tryouts on American Idol. Balancing dreams with reality is critical to business success.

I Will Survive

Running a business is a marathon, not a sprint. At times you may wonder how you'll even put one foot in front of the other. There will be other moments full of jubilant celebration, a sense of invincibility. Like Rock Stars who live for those electric hours on stage, entrepreneurs perpetually seek those triumphs and successes.

I hope this book keeps you moving forward. I hope it has given you an understanding of the drivers behind your profit, and how to manage them to their fullest potential.

Final message from The Numbers Whisperer ™

To your success & happiness -

Nicole

APPENDIX

Finance Rock Star Playlist
pbSmart™ Codes
Kiva.org
Index
Resources
About the Author

Finance Rock Star Playlist

Section	Song or Trivia	Artist(s)
Table of Contents	*Song:* So You Want to be a Rock-n-Roll Star?	The Byrds
	Song: Can't Buy Me Love	The Beatles
	Song: Burning Down the House	Talking Heads
	Song: Dirty Deeds Done Dirt Cheap	AC / DC
	Song: Upgrade U	Beyonce
	Song: Viva Las Vegas	Elvis
	Song: We Will Rock You	Queen
	Song: Dancing on My Own	Robyn
	Song: Glitter	Mariah Carey
Chapter 1	*Trivia:* Suffered from stage fright	Jim Morrison, John Lennon and Eminem
	Song: Lose Yourself	Eminem
	Song: Bringing Sexy Back	Justin Timberlake
Chapter 2	*Trivia:* In 2011 had the top grossing concert tour raking in $195 million.	U2
	Trivia: Musical artists whose success has spanned decades.	Bruce Springsteen, Madonna, U2, The Rolling Stones
	Trivia: Wore a meat dress to the MTV Awards	Lady Gaga
	Trivia: Famously said Van Halen	David Lee Roth
	Trivia: In 2010 was 8th highest paid musician, earning a reported $58 million.	Madonna
Chapter 3	*Trivia:* Musicians with mugshots who continued to have commercial success.	Willie Nelson, 50 Cent, Billie Joe Armstrong (Green Day), Johnny Cash

Section	Song or Trivia	Artist(s)
Chapter 3	*Trivia*: Band that uses just three chords in their songs	The Ramones
	Trivia: Holds the record for the highest average concert ticket price. $306 in 2008.	Elton John
Chapter 4	*Trivia*: Famous American banjo player	Eddie Peabody
	Trivia: Never marketed yet sold out stadiums	The Grateful Dead
	Song: Strangers in the Night	Frank Sinatra
	Song: That's What Friends Are For	Dionne Warwick and Friends
	Song: Walk This Way	Run DMC and Aerosmith
	Trivia: Jim Beam sponsored 2009 Tour	Kid Rock
	Trivia: KC Masterpiece BBQ Sauce and Kingsford Charcoal sponsored 2010 Tour	Keith Urban
	Trivia: Bacardi sponsored 2010 Tour	Black Eyed Peas
	Trivia: Clorox provided tour Brita Water Bar	U2
Chapter 5	*Song:* Life Lessons at the Grocery Store	I admit I made this one up. But doesn't it sound like a Country Western song title?
	Song: Two is Better than One	Taylor Swift
Chapter 6	*Song:* Time is Money	Akon
	Song: Get Yo Groove On	Prince
Chapter 7	*Trivia*: Famous musicians who declared bankruptcy	Jerry Lee Lewis, MC Hammer, Toni Braxton
	Song: Yo Ho Ho and a Bottle of Rum	*Original artist unknown*
	Song: Red, Red Wine	Neil Diamond

Section	Song or Trivia	Artist(s)
	Song: Step by Step	New Kids on the Block
	Song: Stuck on You	Elvis Presley
	Song: Celebration	Kool & The Gang
Chapter 8	*Song*: Rebel Yell	Billy Idol
	Song: Time After Time	Cyndi Lauper
	Trivia: Her touring contract requires a chewing gum disposal attendant be provided	Mariah Carey
	Trivia: Her touring contract requires 25 cases of Kabbalah water be provided	Madonna
	Trivia: Her touring contract requires rose petals in the toilet	Barbara Streisand
	Trivia: Private performance by this group costs seven million dollars	The Rolling Stones
	Trivia: Private performance by this singer costs six and half million dollars	Celine Dion
	Trivia: Private performance by this singer costs three point six million dollars	Christian Aguilera
	Song: It's Tricky	Run DMC
Chapter 9	*Song:* Come As You Are	Nirvana
	Song: The Big Picture	Elton John
	Song: Don't be a Freddie Freeloader	Miles Davis
Chapter 10	*Song:* Pump up the Volume	MARRS
	Song: Haven't I Seen You Before?	Dianne Reeves
Chapter 11	*Trivia:* Famous Las Vegas Acts	The Rat Pack (Frank Sinatra, Dean Martin, Sammy Davis Jr. and Joey Bishop), Elvis and Celine Dion

Rock Star Playlist

Section	Song or Trivia	Artist(s)
	Song: Get Ready	The Temptations
	Song: The Gambler	Kenny Rogers
	Song: Luck Be a Lady	Frank Sinatra
Chapter 12	*Song:* We Will Rock You!	Queen
Chapter 13	*Song:* Dancing on My Own	Robyn
	Song: Make Me Over	Hole
	Song: Taxman	The Beatles
Chapter 14	*Trivia:* Starred in the flop Glitter	Mariah Carey
	Song: I'm Not Dead	Pink
	Song: I Will Survive	Gloria Gaynor

pbSmart™ Codes

Engage your customers with QR codes and custom mobile pages.

Campaigns utilizing QR code and mobile technology are extremely effective in engaging prospects, cross-selling customers and building customer loyalty. See how easy it is to turn direct mail, a poster or a finance book into a unique interactive customer experience.

Quickly generate a QR code that links to a custom mobile web page, YouTube video, vCard, phone number or any URL you select. You'll even be able to track the number of scans and emails you capture.

Use our custom mobile page to:

- Conduct a mobile survey
- Provide a coupon
- Show a video
- Connect to Facebook and Twitter
- Capture email leads
- Provide your website

Scan to get
pbSmart Codes
FREE

Learn more at:

www.pbsmartcodes.com

Kiva.org
Helping Others in True Rock Star Fashion

If you reflect on the big name stars mentioned in this book, you will realize many have used their celebrity to help others. Their causes run the gamut from fighting AIDs to clean water initiatives.

In countries around the globe lack of capital, even a sum as little as $25, keeps many living in poverty from pursuing their dreams. Everyone should have the chance to improve their life, and we want to help make that happen. **Therefore for every copy of this book sold, $1 will be donated to Kiva.org for funding microloans.**

Kiva is a non-profit organization with a mission to connect people through lending to alleviate poverty. Leveraging the internet and a worldwide network of microfinance institutions, Kiva lets individuals lend as little as $25 to help create opportunity around the world.

Do you want to help too?

Visit http://www.kiva.org today and make it happen.

Finance Rock Star Resources

www.FinanceRockStar.com

The official website for *How to be a Finance Rock Star*. Get the latest news, contests, reviews and more.

www.TheNumbersWhisperer.com

This is the place for all things related to The Numbers Whisperer ™. Catch Nicole's latest blog post, radio show or video. Learn how to work with Nicole. Get access to unique and useful finance tools that will grow your bottom line.

www.RockYourProfits.com

Website for the online eCourse offered by Nicole Fende, The Numbers Whisperer™. Cost effective and fun way to dig deeper into the ideas and techniques presented in this book.

www.SmallBusinessFinanceForum.com

The website that started it all. This is the home for Small Business Finance Forum LLC, the umbrella organization for all of Nicole's endeavors. Small Business Finance Forum is also the publisher for *How to be a Finance Rock Star*. If you are considering a book on small business finance we'd love to hear about it!

Connect with Nicole on Social Media

Twitter: http://www.Twitter.com/NicoleAFende

Facebook: http://www.Facebook.com/SmallBizFinance

LinkedIn: http://www.LinkedIn.com/in/nfende

Google +: http://plus.google.com/112340090288262892220

YouTube: http://www.YouTube.com/SmallBizFinance

SmallBizFinance Radio Show

Listen Live Wednesdays at 11 a.m. Central Standard Time: http://www.BlogTalkRadio.com/SmallBizFinance

iTunes Podcast: http://itunes.apple.com/us/podcast/smallbizfinance-blog-talk/id394412159

Listen Online to Past Episodes: http://thenumberswhisperer.com/category/radio/

Index

50 Cent, 28
Aerosmith, 49
Aguilera, Christine, 89
Armstrong, Billie Joe, 28
Avatar
    Fear, 11
    Client, 50
Axe Murderer (Serial Profit Killer)
    Introduction, 11
    Profit Pitfalls, 29, 53, 67, 79, 91, 103, 127
Bacardi, 50
Barter
    Ground Rules, 53
    Resources, 52
    Traditional, 51
    Triangle, 52
    With Strangers, 52
Bartercard.com, 52
Beach, Jim, 46
Beasley, David, 46
BizStats.com, 87
Black Eyed Peas, 50
Braxton, Toni, 69
Budgeting
    Assessing Risk, 112, 114 – 117
    Marketing Example, 112 - 121
    Opportunity Analysis, 114
    Technique, 111 – 112
    Unplanned Opportunities, 117
    Worksheet, blank, 113
Carey, Mariah, 87, 137 - 140
Cash, Johnny, 28
Certified Public Accountant (CPA), 134 - 135
Chatzky, Jean, 41
Cher,
Chill Pills, 19 – 20
Clorox, 50
Comebacks 138 - 140
Crowd Funding, 42 – 44
CrowdCube.com, 48
Customer Funding, 44 – 46
Dion, Celine, 89, 112
eBay, 40 -41
Efficiency Ratio, 28 - 30
Elvis
    Impersonators, 21, 49
    Las Vegas, 112
Eminem, 9, 97
Enrolled Agent, 134 - 135
Entrepreneur Equation (The), 22

Expenses
- Classifying, 73 - 74
- Cost of unreported expenses, 70
- Fixed Expenses, 77, 90 - 91
- Predicting, 78 – 80
- Step Expenses, 75 – 76, 91, 94 - 95
- Tracking Tools, 72
- Variable, 74 -75

Expensify.com, 72

Finance Dramamine, 9 – 10

Finance Rock Star Casino, 112

Fluffy the Finance Feline
- Images, 16, 24, 26, 28, 33, 39, 44, 60, 78, 90, 111, 131
- Introduction, 16

Formulas, 31,

FundAGeek.com, 44

Glitter, 137

Gobbledygook, 14

Grateful Dead (The), 44

GrowVC.com, 48

Hanks, Chris, 46

Income Goals
- Setting, 22
- Considerations, 23

Inflation, 78

International Reciprocal Trade Association (IRTA), 52

Internal Rate of Return (IRR), 60 – 61

ITEX, 52

Joint Ventures, 49

IPO, 48

Jim Beam, 49

John, Elton, 34,

KC Masterpiece Barbeque Sauce, 49

Keebo.com, 72

Key Metrics
- Expenses, 127
- Revenue, 124 – 125
- Problem Solving, 129 - 131
- Sales, 126
- Setting, 124 – 128
- Tracking, 129

Kia, 49

Kickstarter.com, 43

Kid Rock, 49

King, Stephen, 11

Kingsford Charcoal, 49 – 50

KISS, 124

Kiva.org,

Lady Gaga, 24

Las Vegas, 111

Lee, Jennifer, 19

LendFriend.com, 47

LendingClub.com, 47

Lending Karma.com, 47
Lennon, John, 9
Lewis, Jerry Lee, 69
Madison, WI, 45
Madonna, 24, 25, 87, 97, 140
Manufacturer or Producer, 33
Mascots, 15 – 16
Max the Math Mutt
    Introduction, 11
    Helpful Hints, 32, 135
    Images, 16, 22, 32, 42, 46, 60, 66, 71, 84, 107, 117, 135
    Introduction, 16
    No Bull Corner, 22, 42, 50, 107
MC Hammer, 69
More Magazine, 41
Morrison, Jim, 9, 12
Neat.com, 72
Nelson, Willie, 28
Nirvana, 97
Number Muncher
    Images, 11, 48, 57, 63, 106
    Introduction, 11
Pay Per Click Ads Analysis, 115
pbSmart™ Codes, 6
Peabody, Earl, 39
Peer to Peer Lending, 46 - 47
Peerbackers.com, 43

Pricing
    Allocating Fixed Expenses, 90 – 91
    Art vs. Science, 94 - 95
    Basic Components, 83
    Calculate Minimum Price, 92
    Calculating Step Expenses, 91
    Company Profit Goals, 87
    Cost of Time, 84 – 85
    Expenses, 87 – 88
    Predicting Sales Volume, 89 – 90
    Sales, Cost of, 105 – 106
    Sales, Including in Price, 106 - 108
    Total Company, 98 - 99
Profit Formula
    Application 32 -
    Formula, 31
    Introduction, 27
Prosper.com, 47
Quarter Conundrum, 55 - 56
QR Codes, 5 – 6, 35, 40, 69, 105, 121, 141, 149
Ramones, 31
Rat Pack, 111
Reece, Dr. Shannon, 10
RescueTime.com, 30
Return on Investment (ROI)
    Case Study, 57 – 60

  Definition, 57
  Formula, 57
Return on Time Invested (ROTI)
  Case Study, 64 - 67
  Cheat Sheet, 67
  Definition, 64
Right Brain Business Plan™, 19
Rock Your Profits Course, 26, 45
Rolling Stones (The), 24, 89
Roth, Carol, 22
Roth, David Lee, 25
Run DMC, 49
SBA.gov, 134
School for Startups, 46
Score.org, 134
Sell a Band, 43
Service Provider, 32
Shoeboxed.com, 72
Sinatra, Frank, 111
Society of Actuaries, 1
Springsteen, Bruce, 24
Sponsorships, 49 – 50
Streisand, Barbara, 87, 133
Trade Show Analysis, 114
Traditional Media Ads Analysis, 116
U2, 22, 24, 50
U-Exchange, 52
Underwear Option, 12

Urban, Keith, 49 – 50
Van Halen, 25
Villains, 11
Walker, Jennifer "Scraps", 4
What Not To Wear, 133
Work Week Goals, 24
Worksheets
  Allocating Fixed Expenses, 90
  Boredom Busting Budget Planner(Blank), 113
  Boredom Busting Budget Planner (Example), 119
  Company Product Portfolio (Blank), 100
  Company Product Portfolio (Example), 102
  Key Metrics, Expenses (Blank) 127
  Key Metrics, Revenue (Blank), 124
  Key Metrics, Sales (Blank), 126
  Key Metrics, Total Company, 128
  Pricing Single Product (Blank), 86
  Pricing Single Product (Example), 93
Vacation Goals, 24
Van's, 49
VIP Bonuses, 43, 61

About the Author

Nicole Fende is The Numbers Whisperer® and President of Small Business Finance Forum. As a credentialed actuary with experience as a Chief Financial Officer, Investment Banker, and successful entrepreneur, Fende helps her clients reach their profit goals and learn how to effectively and enjoyably run the financial side of their business.

Nicole hosts the well acclaimed weekly SmallBizFinance Show on BlogTalk Radio, delivering tricks and expert interviews to help her listeners improve their bottom line.

Despite Ms. Fende's endless list of impressive credentials, her true claim to fame is her ability to make finance fun. From her laugh out loud blog posts, such as "How College Keggers Teach Complex Expense Analysis", to the endearing finance mascot Fluffy, she entertains entrepreneurs while helping them grown their bottom line.

Nicole lives in the Twin Cities with her husband Paul, daughter Sarah, two lazy cats, and one hyper Irish Setter.

Made in the USA
Middletown, DE
04 April 2016